M000169439

To my family,

The Brummit's

(1844—present)

TALLADEGA DAYS

The biography of William H. Brummit, M.D.,
Civil Rights Activist, Forgotten Legend and
KKK Survivor

A BIOGRAPHY

BY

Houston Brummit, M.D.

Talladega Days
Race, Rural Life, and Memories of a
Forgotten Legend and Kkk Survivor
Copyright © 2021 by Houston Brummit

All rights reserved. No part of this publication may be reproduced, distributed, or transmitted in any form or by any means, including photocopying, recording, or other electronic or mechanical methods, without the prior written permission of the publisher or author, except in the case of brief quotations embodied in critical reviews and certain other noncommercial uses permitted by copyright law.

Although every precaution has been taken to verify the accuracy of the information contained herein, the author and publisher assume no responsibility for any errors or omissions. No liability is assumed for damages that may result from the use of information contained within.

Library of Congress Control Number: 2020906238
ISBN-13:   Paperback: 978-1-64749-097-3
             ePub: 978-1-64749-098-0
             Hardcover   978-1-64749-099-7

Printed in the United States of America

GoToPublish LLC
1-888-337-1724
www.gotopublish.com
info@gotopublish.com

Contents

Photographs

Maps and Special Text

Genealogical Chart

The Brummit(t) Family Tree

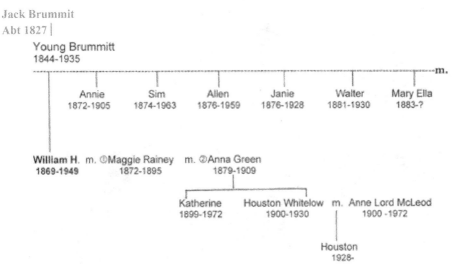

Jack Brummit
Abt 1827

Young Brummitt
1844-1935

| Annie | Sim | Allen | Janie | Walter | Mary Ella |
| 1872-1905 | 1874-1963 | 1876-1959 | 1876-1928 | 1881-1930 | 1883-? |

m.

William H. m. ①Maggie Rainey   m. ②Anna Green
1869-1949   1872-1895   1879-1909

Katherine   Houston Whitelow   m. Anne Lord McLeod
1899-1972   1900-1930   1900 -1972

Houston
1928-

The Brummit(t) Family Tree

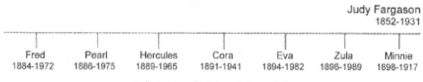

Judy Fargason
1852-1931

Fred	Pearl	Hercules	Cora	Eva	Zula	Minnie
1884-1972	1886-1975	1889-1965	1891-1941	1894-1982	1896-1989	1898-1917

(Infant deaths: Beatrice and Alexander)

m. ③Olla Orr
1893-1978

Martha Jean
1933-

Author's Note

What I learned about my grandfather, William H. Brummit, M.D., came mostly by speaking with his daughter, my Aunt Katherine, and reading the few surviving letters he had written to her. I also learned about him by interviewing Olla Brummit, his widow and third wife; Martha Brummit Peters, his adopted daughter; Pearl Brummit Smith, my great Aunt; Emily Abbott, Pearl's daughter; and Josephine Burton, Dr. Brummit's office aide in Talladega. I primarily benefited from a six-page history on the Brummit family compiled in 1979 by Zula Brummit Campfield, my great Aunt. From her comprehensive history, I have included only those narrative accounts most pertinent to my grandfather.

The deaths of my mother and Aunt Katherine in 1972 freed me from emotional constraints that were inhibiting me from interviewing Olla and Martha. My pursuit to understand my grandfather—who he was, his character and his relationship with my own father, his son—also brought me in closer contact with Aunt Pearl and Cousin Emily. Additionally, I have included writings of Mildred McLeod, my Aunt and mother's younger sister, who describes arduous farm life in Wilsonville, Alabama. It can be assumed that the life she depicts is comparable to that experienced by my grandfather at Camp Hill, Alabama, where he grew up. I am grateful that this quest for information on my grandfather has expanded my inner circle of family. They were invaluable sources and allowed this biography to be told in various voices other than my own.

The notes and recorded interviews were compiled thirty-five years ago during a summer vacation in 1973. Back then, the resulting 200-plus, typed, transcribed pages seemed so daunting that I laid my research aside for a more convenient time; that "more convenient time" came in 2008.

In revisiting the transcriptions, I realized that it was imperative to take some liberties with my familial sources. The most obvious is the virtual elimination of quotation marks. This was done in order to edit generously for the purpose of optimizing clarity. Also, I needed to correct confusion in pronoun usage; strengthen the narrative by reordering the transcribed statements of the contributing sources; and update archaic, century-old expressions for the twenty-first century reader. These enhancements were sensitively executed so to maintain the speaker's voice and intention.

Lastly, as my grandfather had died more than half a century before the writing of this biography, the only direct references that have survived are his letters to Katherine and the text of his speech delivered in the 1940s.

Houston Brummit
March 15, 2020

TALLADEGA DAYS

The biography of William H. Brummit, M.D.,
Civil Rights Activist, Forgotten Legend
and KKK Survivor

We should never cease crying, fighting, and agitating
until this last bar of color has been broken
and our group can come before the world as other people,
to control and market our wares to the world.

WILLIAM H. BRUMMIT, M.D.

William Henry Harrison Brummit, M.D.

1869—1949

Part I

The Brummits:

Race Mixing in Talladega, Alabama

Young and Judy Fargason Brummitt

Houston Brummit:

Many years ago, when I was a student at Meharry Medical College in Nashville, Tennessee, a curious thing happened. I was on my way to my first class when I saw a portly, seemingly white stranger sitting on a porch, playing hillbilly songs on an electric guitar that resounded up and down Jefferson Avenue at Eighteenth Street. He called me over and told me that he was my great-uncle. His name was Josephus Green Jr. and he was the brother of my grandmother, Anna Green, my grandfather's second wife, and Mattie Green. It seems that Mattie Green's son, Flem Otey Jr. owned the grocery store on Jefferson Avenue where Uncle Joe played his guitar. I knew the Oteys, who lived above the market, but I had no idea I was related to them. Uncle Joe was a Negro, yet so fair and with such European features and auburn-colored, straight hair that he could "pass for white"—as many freed slaves and first-generation African Americans did in post-Civil War America. This phenomenon of the "white-colored" Negro was also apparent on my grandfather's side.

The nature of small-town, Southern living combined with the unmentionable reality of white-instigated race mixing created a strange atmosphere wherein the Brummits, both black and white, were forbidden by law to engage in traditional societal norms and rites. Legal marriage, therefore, was taboo. Fraternizing with whites was a form of tightrope artistry, and black men, particularly, were targets of Klan terrorism if they crossed political, economic, and social lines. Oddly enough, my great-grandfather, Young Brummitt, and his children seemingly managed to "enjoy" a certain kind of independence in their interactions with their white relatives.

Zula:

Young Brummitt, my father, was born in 1844 in Mound Bayou, Alabama, as a slave owned by the *white* Brummit family. He worked most of the time in the Brummit house, as he must have been too young to work on the farm. He married Judy Fargason, when she was about thirteen years old. To that union were born sixteen children, two died in infancy. His firstborn was William Henry Harrison Brummit, who would later become a doctor and practice in Talladega.

Olla:

There were so many of them and their relatives. The father, Young, was mixed up with the *white* Brummit family and the mother, Judy Fargason, too. I knew them. You see *her* father was white and *his* father was white and had children with this Negro woman. And you know what their personalities were like with both William's father and grandfather. William was telling me about the way it was with a lot of white families that they were related to; he wouldn't obey. He'd take all what his white relatives had to say because they were all his kinfolks, you know. But they would never do anything to him. He was one of them.

Zula:

Papa farmed on halves for a while. That means that you worked someone else's land, and they furnished you seed and fertilizer and enough money to live on until your crop was harvested. Then you had to give that person half of your crops. The most common term is sharecropping. Papa said he couldn't stand that kind of living, so he started buying land and finally owned one hundred sixty acres. The land that he had in Camp Hill was given to his mother, Ann, who was owned by the Brummits. We did not live on the farm, as it was about two miles from home. So we would ride a wagon or a mule back and forth, to and from the farm.

Olla:

In Talladega, William saw that there were white families all over the city, and one was the Brummits, and one of them was a doctor. William's mother's people, the Fargasons, were the smartest. They were all white, too. You see, your great-grandmothers both came from white fathers. William told me this because they all grew up together and knew each other and all married a kinship.

When your grandfather was quite a big boy, the *white* Brummits were going to hire some of their relatives, the *black* Brummits, for help. When William got there, the *white* Brummits said they could tell your grandfather was related to them. He wanted to hire William, but they couldn't because they knew that, as he was a relative, they couldn't order him around and mistreat him. Also, the *white* Brummits had experienced a lot of trouble with Young Brummitt, his father, his children, and his cousins, and all up through the black-white mixtures.

Houston Brummit:

Jack Brummit was both the father and slave owner of Young Brummitt. To differentiate himself, Young added a "t" to his last name. However, my grandfather William H. decided to keep the original spelling of his family name and removed the second "t".

Part II

Rural Life in the Childhood Home of William H. Brummit

State Map of Alabama

with designated counties
significant in the life of
William H. Brummit

Camp Hill, as remembered by Aunt Zula

Houston Brummit:

Judy Fargason Brummitt within thirty years birthed sixteen children with two dying in infancy. William H. Brummit, her first child was much older than his siblings. Consequently, they did not have an opportunity to know him. At the age of twenty he left the farm to pursue an education. It is reasonable to believe that he performed the same difficult chores described by Aunt Zula

Much of the farm work that he had undertaken now fell to his younger brothers Sim, Allen, Walter, and Fred, all of whom had grown capable enough to shoulder the arduous physical farm responsibilities William had inevitably inherited as the oldest son.

Young Brummitt, a former slave, spelled the family name with two "*t*"s. Some of his descendants deferred to Young Brummitt by retaining the double-*t* spelling; others used a single-*t* spelling, which Aunt Zula thought was the original spelling of the family name.

The following oral history describes growing up in rural Alabama and the day-to-day experiences from which emerged my grandfather, William H. Brummit, who was thirty years Zula's senior.

Zula:

They called me "Boot," and I was born August 4, 1896, in Camp Hill, Alabama. Camp Hill is a small town of 1,500 people located in the southeastern part of the state near the Georgia border in Tallapoosa County. The nearest big city is Columbus, Georgia, and next in size would be Opelika, Alabama, where most people went for surgery at Lee County Hospital. When I was growing up there, they had two doctors and a dentist. They had a black mayor, Mr. Frank Holley. The city council was made up of three blacks and two whites. The blacks had two churches: the Murray Chapel A. M. E. Zion Church, pastored by Reverend Lonnie Smith; and Mount Lonely Missionary Baptist Church, pastored by Reverend Willie Smith. Both churches are up to date with organ, piano, nice pews, a kitchen, and air conditioning. The whites had three churches: Methodist, Baptist, and Presbyterian.

The Camp Hill population was about sixty percent black. There was a park and recreation center over by the Baptist Church that had tennis courts, softball, and baseball fields, but no swimming pool. The center was built by the federal and local governments. There were some new apartments for low income that were integrated. I don't think they had any kind of park or playground. The whites would never let any kind of industry come there, which, most likely, would have been cotton mills. They didn't want their children to go to school with mill children. Most of their children went to the Southern Institute until they built a school in town. Most of the black people tried to send their children to school. When they finished what was offered in Camp Hill, they sent them off to school. The school there now is very nice, but it is too far out from Camp Hill and most of the homes.

We only had one black school there and that was the Edward Bell High School. Mr. George Ervin was the principal. He was black. About 2 percent of the teachers were white. There were no white pupils at all. There were five grocery stores owned by whites, and two owned by blacks. There were two clothing stores owned by whites and one bank, the Camp Hill Bank. They had a city hall that housed the fire department and quarters for the city council meetings. Black business was, most time, a pressing and cleaning shop with a restaurant. It was located in the basement of a store on the main street with the opening in back to the railroad tracks. A Mr. Lum Heard had a grocery store that was on the street that went to the gin house. He and his family left Camp Hill and opened a store in Chattanooga, Tennessee. My brother-in-law, Arthur, had a cleaning business for a while along with some farming. I think he sold out to Frank Pullum when he left his family for Port Huron. In 1924, Cora Brummit and her husband, Arthur Spigner, brother of Sheppie Spigner-Bennett, moved from Camp Hill, Alabama, to Port Huron, Michigan, with five children: Douglas, Bernice, Doris, Eva, and Fletcher. Two other children, Sheppie and Carlos, were born in Port Huron.

When we were growing up, most of the entertainment centered around churches and school. We went to church suppers and parties in people's homes. On Sunday we would go to Sunday school and church. In the evening we would go to the railroad station to see the six o'clock train go by and walk home with our boyfriends, and they would stay until time to go to church at night.

I can recall several instances of racial happenings. The first I remember is when a black man was working on a white man's farm and the white man's wife had a baby by the black man. He was the brother of our friend, Ophelia. I never did know what happened to her brother.

Another incident was where a black man disappeared when a white man's cows got into his corn patch and the black man killed one of the cows. I don't know what happened to him. Then one Sunday one of the young men, who lived close to us, hired a horse and buggy to take his girlfriend for a ride, but when he got to her house, he was so drunk she wouldn't go with him. So he beat the horse up, and it ran off the bridge down onto the railroad tracks. He took the horse and buggy back to the stable and went home. In a few minutes here comes the white man up the lane, and he went and shot the boy in the leg. The boy was living with his grandfather and he sent him away. I don't know where.

Another black boy had to leave because a white girl said he made a nasty proposal to her in the alley in back of her father's store. I know he went to Louisville to some of his relatives. He was just a kid. This girl's brother told Ernest Holley, an older boy, that he was telling a lie and Ernest slapped him down, and Ernest really had to make a run for it. He ran through the woods to a train stop called Slaughter's Crossing, and one of the ladies that lived there locked him in her house so he could leave his home and catch a freight train. He is living in Detroit, but his family stayed in Camp Hill until his mother was almost a hundred years old. He goes back to Camp Hill any time now. Most of the trouble was caused by some new white people who came there and opened a store. In fact they practically took over Camp Hill. So I think the other white people were just as glad to see them leave as the blacks were.

Another occurrence that was interesting was when Miss Emma and Anna Jarrell lived across the street from us and had a military store. They had a brother named Luke who was a farmer, and he brought a little black boy home with the name of Early. I think they loved and reared Early like they would a puppy. He had a pallet in the house where he slept. Luke married a beautiful woman much younger than he. She and Early would play, and if she would hit him, you could hear him yelling a mile away, saying, "Miss Lucille hit me." Luke had built them a new house down in the town and took Early with them as he was a big boy now and could work on the farm. Seems like he saw Miss Lucille do something that he didn't think was right, so he told Mr. Luke and they separated. Shortly afterward, Early died, and they say Mr. Luke would go down on the farm and see Early's tracks, where he had plowed, and he would break down and weep. In a short time, he died and everyone said from grieving over losing his wife and then Early. That's the way colored folks told it.

The last incident I know of is when the farmers were trying to unionize to get better prices for their crops and the whites said the unionizers were communists. One night they were having a meeting at a schoolhouse, and they had a man out watching. A band of whites with the sheriff raided the schoolhouse and killed the watchman and put the others in jail. That ended the farmers trying to better their conditions. At that time everything the blacks would try to do, like help themselves, was called "communist," and I am sure that no one of us knew what a communist was.

As far back as I can remember, Jane Fargason, or Granny, my maternal grandmother, lived in a one-room house in back of our house. Her slave owners had brought her from South Carolina. She had two real high beds and a trunk where she had her quilts and sheets folded on top. She cooked on the fireplace and she had two skillets that you would make a fire under. When the wood would burn into coals, she would put some hot coals on the top lid to brown the bread on top. I don't remember her working, so Mama and Papa must have been taking care of her. She was able to see enough to make quilts.

After she became a little feeble, Mama would make one of us children spend the night with her. We would fuss because we would be by ourselves with her and the other children would be out playing and having fun. When Papa built a bigger house up the lane, Mama would bring Granny up there to stay. But every time she got mad, she would go back home. It was very dangerous for her to try to make fires. She was so very cold-natured that you had to have a fire all night. One day while Allen and Papa were working the garden, Granny's house burned down. I have always thought maybe they had to burn it down as it was just a falling-down shack and you couldn't keep her out of it when she got mad. I thought she was going to have a stroke when she looked out the window and saw her house on fire, but she had to live with us from then on, which was a long time.

One of us would have to sleep in the room with her to keep the fire going in the fireplace. When she would get cold, we would have to make hot coffee in a boiler over the coals. She would have so many quilts on the bed that she could hardly turn over. She had that trunk in which she kept her things. If she got real mad, she would slip off and go over to the white woman's house, Mrs. Janie Clark, and sit on the front steps and tell how she was being mistreated.

Mama would have to go over and bring her home. She would almost have to drag her and she would be fussing every step of the way. She finally lost her sight, and because none of us was home all the time, Mama moved her into the room with her and Papa. After a while she became very ill and went into a coma. Bernice and Doris were living next door. When they heard that Granny was dying, they came and walked around the bed and said, "Goodbye, Granny." Since she said she remembered "the stars that fell over Alabama," they figured she must have been around 115 years old when she died. She had three daughters: Aunt Mollie, Aunt Mamie, and my mother, Judy, a host of grandchildren and great-grandchildren. She was the second person to be buried in the family cemetery—around 1916.

Houston Brummit:

The *stars that fell over Alabama,* in fact, were not stars but thousands of meteors. This spectacular meteor shower occurred over Alabamian skies in 1833, and Jane Fargason had witnessed the phenomenon.

Zula:

These are things we had to do to raise a crop. First, we would put out the manure that had accumulated in the barn during the winter where the mules and cows were kept. If you intended to put new land into cultivation, you had to cut off the brush and pull up the tree stumps. Next, you had to break up your land with a plow and lay out rows to put in your commercial fertilizer that we called guano. Then, after it was settled for a while, you were ready to plant your corn, cotton, and oats. We also raised sugar cane, watermelons, and peanuts. We dropped the seed corn by hand, but had a planter that dropped the cottonseeds. Next would be chopping cotton to thin it out and get the weeds and grass out of it. Most times you had to plow it twice and hoe it twice. When July came, it was what we called "laying by time," so we would have a few weeks' rest before it was time to pick the cotton and pull the corn. Papa would then go to the gin house where the cotton was run through machinery to separate the cotton from the seeds and the cotton was made into bales. Papa was head of the ginning department, and Sim and Allen worked there, too. We children would have to carry dinner to the gin house, and they would give us a penny or a nickel for bringing the dinner and we bought candy with it.

After the cotton was picked, we would get ready to make syrup. First, we stripped the leaves off the cane, then we cut down the stalks and carried them to the mill where a mule was hitched to a pole. He went round and round while you fed the cane into the mill that had pressers that pressed the juice out of the cane. The juice was then carried to a pan that was set on a foundation of stone where wood was burning to cook the juice into syrup. The pan was divided so that when the juice would boil you could pass it on to another, taking off what we called "skimmings," until when it got to the last division of the pan, where it would come out beautiful sugar cane syrup to be put into gallon tin buckets. Most times we would have a hundred or more gallons. Sometimes Papa would sell some of it. Sim was the syrup maker, with all of us helping. Papa was there overseeing everything.

After all of us left home, Papa started renting land and re-renting it to some of the black farmers who did not own land and didn't have the money to pay rent. They would pay him off when they harvested their crops. Some of the grandsons would stay with them and work at the Southern College and pay them for their room and board. They also rented out part of the house. He gave most of us (Fred, Janie, Walter, Cora, and myself) some kind of home. He had a little cash money and he gave a small amount to Sim, Allen, and Pearl. The eighty acres of land he left for Bud and Eva. He read the Bible a great deal and he came across the passage, "He that doesn't provide for his family is worse than an infidel." I may not have quoted exactly what is in the Bible, but I am saying that he was determined to give all of his children something.

After Mama died in 1931, one of Fred's daughters lived with our father for a while along with one of Walter and Sim's daughters. Then when he became real sick, Pearl went down from Goodwater, and I went down to relieve her and stayed about a month until he died in August 1935 at the age of ninety-one. He was survived by nine children and a host of grand, great-grand and great-great-grandchildren. He had served God, family, and the community well. He was a member of Spring Hill Primitive Baptist Church.

Any time there was any racial trouble in Camp Hill, the whites would always come around to him first. When my father was sick, a lot of whites came to see him. One said if there had been electricity in the house, he would have given him an electric fan, because his breath was very short as he suffered from emphysema. Mr. Ward, the president of the Southern College, brought some beautiful roses to the house and read a poem at his funeral. As I said, the land Papa owned in town was given to his mother by "Old Man Brummit." The original way to spell our name was B-r-u-m-m-i-t, with one "*t*".

Judy Fargason Brummitt, our mother, was born in Camp Hill. We always lived in the same neighborhood as some white and black Fargason or their relatives. There was a Fargason descendant living on the corner of Brummit Street and Main Street.

The first remembrance I have of Mama was her taking in washing and ironing. We would have to go and get the dirty clothes. She would give them back when they were washed and ironed, and we would have to go to the back door. Mama was very careful how she washed clothes. She would have them all separated in three piles—the whites, the near-whites, and the colored. She would wash the whites and put them in a black iron pot to boil, then take them out to put them on the battling block to be batted with a paddle, and rinsed through three waters with the last rinse with bluing in it. All of the water had to be hand drawn from a well.

She always had some children in the house besides her own to take care of. When her oldest daughter died, she took in her two children. The father later took the boy for a short time, but she kept the girl until she got married. When Anna Green died, the second wife of her oldest son, William Henry Harrison, Mama kept his two children, Houston Whitelow and Katherine, until he could get settled. There was a Buddy and an Annie who stayed there most of the time while their mother worked. They were not related to us but lived nearby.

Papa ran the farm and Mama ran the house and garden. Papa or one of my brothers would break up the soil in the garden, and she, along with us, would do the planting and cultivating. She had a church member and friend, Aunt Vee Russell, who had a big fruit orchard and we would go get the fruit for her to can. We had lots of fig preserves.

Houston Brummit:

Canning fruit and vegetables was a food process that my mother often carried out until I attended college. She would heat peaches, strawberries, and other fruits and vegetables until they boiled. The hot compote was poured into clear, green-glass Mason jars and covered with melted paraffin. Then a rubber seal was placed around the edge of the jar and a metal lid with a porcelain undercoating screwed down to the rubber seal. The process preserved vegetables and fruits for long-term storage; jellies and jams were also typical end products. When grapes were put through the same process and sugar added, the end product was grape juice that had to be strained through porous cloth. Occasionally, the juice fermented and became an acidic wine.

Seven of the sixteen Brummit siblings.
From left to right: Minnie, Zula, Sim, Allen, (Huff, Pearl's
husband), Bud, Pearl, and Fred

Zula:

She had to churn the milk and see that the hogs were slopped. Most times, there were two calves tied out to graze and they would have to be watered. When time came to gin the cotton, she would have to fix something for dinner to send to the gin house. When we worked in the fields, she would have to cook the dinner and pack it in buckets for us young-uns to carry to the fields. We also had two or three small patches of sweet potatoes that were near the house. We would have to set out the plants and water them until they took root if it didn't rain. In the fall Papa would plow them up, and we would have to pick them up, put them in piles to haul to the house in a wagon, and bed them down in the ground with corn shucks surrounding them, and cover them with dirt to keep for the winter. They would have to be gathered before the first frost fell.

When winter came, Mama would have made us two outing underskirts, two pairs of panties made out of sheeting, and two dresses. I don't know how she made them before Allen married Minnie who was a good seamstress and made most of our clothes.

We would get two pairs of stockings, two pairs of long underwear, and a pair of shoes. The older ones of us would get more. We all had some kind of jacket or coat. We took a bath once a week in the winter and changed clothes once a week. In the summer we could play in the creek and get caught in the rain coming home from the farm, so I guess we were much cleaner. Mama would always make us wash our feet when we went barefoot because she always had white sheets on the beds, especially if they were made out of feed sacks. She was a member of Spring Hill Primitive Baptist Church and would go to church on the fourth Saturday and Sunday each month.

For some reason, we never cooked dinner on Sunday, as most Sunday mornings we would have a special breakfast. Papa would buy a piece of cheese on Saturday night and on Sunday morning Mama would cook it with scrambled eggs. That was something extra to go with our syrup, butter, and biscuits. She would always leave a big pan of biscuits for us to eat. We would play baseball and a lot of the neighborhood kids would come. Cora, my older sister, would line us up and give everybody a biscuit and tell us to take our fingers and make a hole in it. She would take the syrup jar and pour syrup in the hole and tell us to run to the end of the porch. Of course, when Mama got home from church there was a regular trail of syrup from the kitchen across the porch, which she would make us wash up. The flies would have been having a picnic. Mama would wear pretty white starched aprons and bonnets. She always kept a grandchild with her. She kept Janie's children while Janie worked. Pearl's daughter, Emily, would come and stay a while, and Cora lived next door and sometimes in the house with her. In later years Jane's son and one of Sim's sons boarded with her while they worked. One of Fred's daughters lived with them until Mama died.

I guess I would to put have to put hog killing time in here as Mama had most of the work to do after the hogs were killed. We generally had two hogs weighing 350 to 500 pounds to kill each winter. You would have to wait until the weather was freezing to kill the hogs. Sim, Fred, and Allen would come early in the morning and we would have an iron pot of boiling water. They would knock the hogs in the head with an axe. Later on they started shooting them in order not to do too much damage to the head. The hogs would squeal and run until they would tumble over a die—not a pretty picture to watch. Then they would douse the hog in hot water and scrape all the hair off. They had a scaffold, and they would put hooks in the hind legs, lift him up, and take a sharp knife and cut down his belly. All the entrails would fall out into a tin tub. Mama and the girls would take all the fat of the entrails to be made into lard. The hog was then cut up and trimmed, taking out the backbone and spare ribs. The lean trimmings would go to make sausage and the fat went to make lard. The meat had to stay out overnight in order to get to the bone. The next day it was salted down in wooden boxes to stay until March or April, when it was taken out and smoked with hickory chips. On the day after the killing we would grind up the sausage, and Mama would have large tin cans and buckets to put the lard in. We would clean some of the small guts to put, the sausage in to make link sausage. Then Mama would boil the hog head, ears, and feet and make souse out of them. When we got through there would be an inch of grease on the kitchen floor.

She made her own soap to wash clothes and for cleaning. We would buy Octagon soap for bathing. She would get a barrel and set it on rocks, and during the winter, when we had fires, we would put the ashes in the barrel. When it was about half full, we would pour water on the ashes and bore a hole near the bottom. She would put a shingle under the hole, and the ashes and water would make lye and it would run down the shingles into a pan. All leftover grease and meat would be mixed with the lye in an iron pot, and Mama would sit and stir until it made soap. Sometimes, she would make soft soap; other times, she would make it hard and cut it into bars to be used for washing dishes. She really ruined her hands by using that strong lye soap.

When Mama and Papa were sick, I would go down there. Mollie and Sim would send milk and butter up to us every day and vegetables out of the garden. Mollie always had the best buttermilk and real yellow butter that I ever tasted. Mollie died before Sim. He lived with one of his daughters for a while until he came home to live with his son, Horace. He finally came to the home place and one of Fred's daughters looked after him until he died in the 1950s. He was way up in years. Sim did more for Mama and Papa than any of us. When Papa was real sick and we had to sit with him, Sim would come around four in the afternoon and sit with me all night. We did this until Papa died.

Sim went to select the casket for Papa and said Papa didn't have quite enough money to get the one he wanted. When Sim said he would pay the difference, I told him to rent out the house and get his money back. Papa left his children some cash money and also some nice land. I don't hear from any of my brothers and sisters.

Our sister, Pearl Brummit Smith, was born in 1886, married at an early age and had one child. That marriage dissolved when her daughter was five months old. She was always a good manager, a hard worker, and with what little money she had, she maintained a pretty nice house and cooked good food. She remarried when her daughter was two years old and the family moved to Goodwater, Alabama.

Because they were very poor, she took in washing and did odd jobs. Her husband took a job hauling logs with a team of four to six oxen. His pay was fifty cents a day. Her income was roughly $2.50 a week. That was in 1907. By 1924, her daughter married, and by 1926 they had purchased a ninety-eight-acre farm outside of town and moved to a four-room cottage. She told me about her religious conversion late in life, and she became a member of Pleasant Home Baptist Church. She enjoyed going to church and paying her assessments.

When Emily became able, she showered Pearl with good things to make life happier for her. Pearl and her husband farmed extensively for many years. Eventually, her daughter graduated from the Chicago Board of Education as a nurse. When Pearl's husband died in 1966, she went to live with Emily in Blue Island, Illinois, and remained there until her death in 1976 at the age of 90. When she died, Emily buried her in the Brummitt Cemetery. Emily still has the farm. The house, where her mother lived, is boarded up with her mother's things just as she left them.

Our brother Hercules, or "Bud," was the tenth living birth. No one ever called him Hercules, and where he got the name, I don't have any idea. I think Bud was born mean and lazy—as far as farm work and school were concerned. The first things I remember about him were at school. We were going to a little log cabin school over at Spring Hill and Mrs. Esther was the teacher. Bud and Son Russell would hang from the rafters anytime they took a notion, and Mrs. Esther couldn't do a thing about it because they were much bigger than she. If any of the other students would do anything she would whip them with a limber hickory switch that she always had plenty of in the corner. I think now she would take her anger out on someone she wasn't afraid of because she was afraid of Son and Bud. I don't think Bud went to school after that and I don't remember him working on the farm because Cora and Zana were doing most of the plowing. He might have been over on Allen's farm.

In the country, they would have a Saturday Night Frolic, and it generally drew a pretty rough crowd. There was a lot of gambling and drinking, and he would go to them. He was flirting with this man's wife and the man was afraid of him, so he went out and shot Bud in the leg through a window. It was not until Sunday early in the morning that Olin brought him home in a one-horse wagon with his leg shot halfway off. He almost died, and did he sing and pray!

The bone was splintered in the leg and it never did heal properly because some of the splinters would work out from time to time. He finally married Viola Benson and they had one child, Clemmie. Papa and the boys got together and built him one of the Brummitt two-room specials up on the side of the hill on Sim's land. He was to farm on Papa's land. He wasn't able to do much farming because that leg gave him trouble. One time when we were making syrup, he went to cut some wood to go into the furnace and cut his foot almost off. He would have his axes as sharp as a razor. When Sim saw all the blood coming out of Bud's foot, he fainted, and we had to pour water over him and rush Bud to the doctor before he bled to death. Of course, we were scared, too, but Old Man Young Brummitt kept his cool and kept things from getting out of hand.

Bud and Viola finally separated, and I remember he started courting a lady named Pearlie. One Saturday evening he came and borrowed Papa and Mama's buggy, and he and Pearlie got into a fight and he shot her. The police came to look for him and they got Allen and Sim to go find him, but I don't remember his ever going to jail.

The next episode was when a white man slapped Cliff, our nephew. Bud waylaid him and almost killed the man by hitting him up side the head with a rock. The police came and told Papa to tell Bud to leave town because by that time he had acquired the name of "Bad Bud Brummit." Papa said this about Bud: "He knows he can't drink whiskey. If you would squeeze a rotten apple up his –hole, he would go somewhere and act the fool."

Bud left Camp Hill and went to Goodwater, where Pearl lived, and I think they finally did put him in jail. When he left Goodwater, he went to Dayton, Ohio, that happened to be where Aunt Eva had moved. That was when a lot of people were leaving the South and going north. He came back to Camp Hill and took Mama back to Dayton. Then he left Dayton and went to Detroit and we didn't hear from him directly for a long time. Some people that would come back visiting said he was making his money putting in culverts on the streets.

Finally the Depression hit and he wrote home to Mama for $25. Mama had about $25 in a tobacco sack pinned in her bosom that she wanted to send to him, but Allen and I said, "No." Allen said if he couldn't make a living in Detroit, there was plenty of land for him to come home and farm. Mama cried and worried over him, but Allen and I did not send him the money. For years we didn't hear anything from him until he showed up in Chicago and started working for Emily. He came with her several times to Nashville to visit me. He told of the hard times and his traveling as a hobo from one place to the other. He never called Mama, Papa, or anyone else.

My first remembrance of home is having a rope swing in a tree in the backyard and I would sit in it for long periods of time. Mama was taking in washing and ironing and she would put an ironing board down low for me to help iron the dry clothes. But I wanted to iron some of the sprinkled clothes, so I got a table napkin, scorched it, and almost got a whipping. I was soon big enough to pick cotton near the house, so if you were not big enough to go to the farm, you could pick in patches. After I got older, Cousin Zana and I used to get up early and go cotton picking; we could pick 300 pounds in a day.

The first teacher I had was Miss Wade in the Missionary Baptist Church, as we didn't have a schoolhouse for a long time. I also went to school at Spring Hill Primitive Baptist Church, where Miss Ester was the teacher. Then I went to school in a house where my brother Walter was a teacher. When I was nine years old, my teacher was Mrs. Leora Herron-Pulliam. The last teacher I had in Camp Hill was Mr. Arthur Doss, and by that time we had a schoolhouse with a nine-month school term so you could finish the eighth grade.

After I finished the eighth grade, I went to A.M. Normal at Normal, Alabama. I finished high school in two years. I took the teacher's examination and got a teacher's license. The first place I taught was helping Miss Tucker at Spring Hill where I made $15 per month. Janie's son used to walk with me three miles each day to school and back. Some days, if it rained hard, we would have to find a place to cross the creek, which meant we would have to walk to a higher bridge.

The next school was Sandy Level, where I was to be an assistant to Mrs. Janie. When she left at Christmas and didn't come back, I became principal and stayed there two years. I can't think of the name of the next school, but for one term Katherine, Dr. Brummit's daughter, was the assistant teacher. I then left Camp Hill and went to Dayton, Ohio, where Eva lived. One of Eva's church members, Lula Knox, was going to Wilberforce University and asked me about going. I made up my mind on the spot, and three weeks later I went with her. I had saved a little money from my teaching and I used it for my entry fees. I worked for the dining room to pay my other expenses. In the summer I worked in the printing shop to get a little spending change. You could stay in the dormitory free, but at night all of the lights would be turned off. I finished Wilberforce in 1921 and went to Augusta, Georgia, to work for the North Carolina Insurance Company. Mr. C. C. Spaulding was head of the district.

I had malaria when I was a child, and it came back on me in Augusta because it was hot and humid, and the mosquitoes would eat you up. I started having nosebleeds every afternoon and became ill, so I had to leave. I went back to Camp Hill and got a job as assistant teacher at Camp Hill City School for a year. Then I got a job in Jacksonville, Florida, with the Pythians. I married John Campfield. He was a linotype operator in the printing department. He started playing "Bolita" and got so far in debt he would have to go a mile out of the way every day to keep from passing where he played. Finally, they got so hot behind him he decided to go to Atlanta, and I decided to go to Nashville. I knew two people there who had been in Wilberforce with me. I went to the YWCA and Mrs. Chavis, the head, told me that a lady was there to try out for a job at the National Baptist Publishing Board and for me to go and try for the job.

When I got to the Publishing House, I found another Wilberforce graduate, who was the cashier. So Mr. Boyd hired us both. Since I had forgotten all the shorthand I had known, I started off as a helper. I took a correspondence course in bookkeeping, so when the bookkeeper quit, I got his job. There I stayed for thirty-five years. I can't say enough good things about Mr. Boyd and the Baptist Publishing House because it gave me a place to settle down and make a good living. Campfield came to Nashville on his way to Phoenix, but I had no intention of leaving Nashville. I thought I had moved around enough, and I could take care of myself. His father came and said he had met Dr. Brummit in Chicago, and he thought John could get a job there as a linotype operator. But the Lord had placed me where I had a good job, and I wasn't going to give it up.

When I look back on my life, I can think of so many failures that I had. Even when I tried some things to help someone else, so many ended in failures because I didn't have enough patience and faith to see things through. I wanted problems to end too quickly. I certainly had more failures than successes. These are some of the things that I feel maybe if I had done differently, maybe I would have been more successful: I should have given more financial support to Mama and Papa; I should have kept my grandniece Greather here with me in Nashville, even if it meant greater sacrifices; I should have tried harder to persuade Herbert to stay here; and I should have tried harder to keep Douglas in school. These are some of my regrets— although I have many more.

Houston Brummit:

This personal history was inserted in the Port Huron brochure upon her family's request, a few years before her death at age 93.

Chapter 2

Camp Hill, as remembered by Aunt Pearl and Cousin Emily

Pearl:

My father's name was Young Brummitt. He was born a slave. That was the white people's name, and that's the name they gave him. He was short, about 5' 6" or something like that. I always thought the sun rose and set on him.

I was crazy about him. I remember everything about him. He hasn't been passed too long ago. He died in 1935. He was a Bible reader who read the Bible a whole lot. My mother was Judy Brummitt, and although she was a very religious person, a Christian, she couldn't read. But Daddy taught himself to read. That's a nice story you can tell about him.

This here slave owner had two kids, a boy and a girl, and they wanted to teach him. He would have to sit down on the hearth and keep a lantern lit for them to see by. We didn't have no electricity or nothing like that in those days. That's the way he learned. When he would hear old man Brummit coming, he would put the books under him. And this slave owner was his father and these two white children, that were doing the studying, were his half-brother and sister. They wanted to teach him. He had to hold the light for them. They got a big thrill out of this because their father didn't want it done. That's how he learned to read and figure and all kinds of stuff. He could figure out a problem in his head faster than the average person could figure it up on paper.

In our home, there was that kind of inward drive to really do something and accomplish whatever you could at that particular time. Of course, the opportunities weren't so great, but I don't think you could say that anybody was really trifling or lazy or didn't want to try to better their position in whatever way they could.

Emily:

We didn't farm nothing but cotton and corn and maybe some oats for the livestock. That's all we had. We just farmed because Granddaddy was the type of person that didn't believe in any of his family working in any white person's house. That's the one thing he didn't believe in. Doctor was along those lines too. You see, I operated a restaurant for my livelihood for about eighteen years. Granddaddy was very proud that we didn't do any servitude work of that sort. It was something that came down through the family. I know there was a large white man that had a white school down there and got after papa to let some of us "to go work in his school." He told the white man to his face, "I ain't got a child that I'm gonna let be *nobody's* servant!" He was very proud.

Oh yeah, I was crazy about him because Granddaddy and Grandmother were the loving kind. I stayed there more than I did at home up until I was about thirteen years of age because they would let you play and have a good time. You could run from the front door to the back door, over and under the beds, just as long as you didn't run through their bedroom. They were the kind where you could just be free and have a good time. Sweet and loveable.

You had plenty of time for recreation together. There was togetherness, and I guess mealtime was one of the times we used to have more fun, because we had a long wooden table and benches on each side, and then everybody'd sit down and have their plate served, and if one ate his food before the others did, Granddaddy'd say, "Look at that over there," and snatch your food when you weren't looking. Then there would be a big scramble. It was always enjoyable at Granddaddy and Grandmama's house.

During the day, everybody that came to town came by their house, came in the back door and went out the front. But I mean everybody passed through that house, family, you know, and grandchildren. The grandchildren were always there, always wanted to go there and always enjoyed being there because there was very little punishment and really, I guess, because of the way that they were towards the children. There was no insubordination; there really was no reason for whipping.

The house looked like a wreck. (*Laughter*). The first house I remember was a big old house. It had two big front rooms and a hall right between them and two back rooms and a porch, one of them long porches, that went all the way across the front, and it faced on the main little road. That street is still there now. That's where they were living when they were attacked with smallpox before the doctors knew what smallpox was.

Granddaddy worked in the cotton gin there, and some white man from up in the hills brought a load of cotton to town; it was too late to get it ginned that evening. That man slept in his cotton that night, and Granddaddy ginned it the next day and came down with this unusual disease. So many of the family, you know, had this disease and the doctors didn't know what it was. It was many years later before they knew anything about smallpox, and I guess we were the first family that had it. I must have been approximately eight years old when I had it. Some of them didn't have it and some did. I don't think there was any who died. I remember that.

Pearl:

I went to school under my brother, William Brummit, when I was about six or seven years old; he must have been around twenty- six. I was going to school, as were the other children, and he was teaching us. It was our public school for about three months, and then we would have to go pick cotton or whatever else that had to be done. Farm work was all there was to do.

Your granddaddy and Uncle Allen worked at the cotton gin. That's how Allen lost his arm. I remember when they were ginning the cotton; the gin took off his arm and left fragments. Doctor hadn't started practicing. He had been to Montgomery and took the state medical examination, but I don't think he had gotten his papers. But he was with Allen at that time. A doctor from Kansas City amputated Allen's arm because your granddaddy didn't have any instruments or things like that at that time.

Chapter 3

Wilsonville, as described by Aunt Mildred McLeod

Corroborating the ruggedness of Alabama farm life is the following 1973 letter written to me by my aunt, Mildred McLeod, my mother's sister. Their father and uncles farmed their grandfather's plantation outside of Wilsonville, sixty miles away from the Brummitt farm, and were the friends and peers of Dr. W. H. Brummit.

Thursday Morning

Dear Houston:

It seems that I just can't settle down and keep my promise—just lazy. Don't think for once that my love for you has diminished one bit. I am in love with my family.

Here are a few lines of information about the McLeod background. Very simple and commonplace but to me it was beautiful to be in the family—my memories are so vivid of the good life made possible for me because of them. The grandparents, Anne and Erasmus McLeod, who were freed slaves, were parents of four sons: Grandville, John, Thomas (your grandfather), and Abraham McLeod. There was one girl, Maggie, who died at 22 years of age. Maggie, John, and Thomas attended Talladega College for two years.

When our grandparents were freed, they were given a homestead by their former slave masters and enough land, 10 acres, to make a living. On the land was a log cabin with one large room and a kitchen. It was deep down in the woods. The surroundings were beautiful: trees and trees and trees. After the death of our grandparents, the three brothers, who were honest, ambitious, hard workers, bought up any land that was available. The brothers owned over 1000 acres but I can't say exactly how much more. It could be a total of 1500 acres including some valuable land on the Cassa River. John never married.

Grandville and Thomas did. Grandville had two children, boy and a girl. The boy died early. Thomas had five children: four by our mother, Lavinia, and one in a second marriage.

The three brothers worked together, helping out each other when and where they were needed. Their lives on the farm were hard and well programmed. Every morning they were up at 2:30 A.M. to feed the cattle and milk the cows. They had many cows, horses and mules and all kinds of fowl. They took 30 minutes off for lunch. The only rest days were Sundays and the bad rainy ones.

As I listened to their conversations, it was strictly business and how to get plows in an environment that was hostile if you were inclined to progress too far. The white people respected the McLeod boys, as they were called, but the McLeods knew very well that they were black and had to walk cautiously to stay around. This they did. They did nothing to offend the whites. They always spoke politely and humbly to them. Back there this was the only way to survive.

The main means of making a living in their days on the farm was selling cotton. But our father, Thomas, made money selling farm products, such as vegetables from his garden, fruits from a large orchard: pears, apples, plums, strawberries, and from Uncle John's garden: peanuts, watermelon, cantaloupes, etc. He also sold milk cows and calves, chickens, turkeys, guineas and eggs. They made hundreds of gallons of syrup from river cane.

The three brothers, though humble, would speak their peace when the white man was not overhearing. They were alert and conveyed much through their eyes and actions. There was no school for black children to attend so the brothers built one on the farm. It was burned down on several occasions by the whites. The last one became a part of the Shelby County School System. The brothers wanted all to get as much education as possible.

Thomas McLeod's first wife was from Talladega and they sent their children to Talladega College. Our father and Dr. Brummit were good friends because they went to Talladega together. Uncle Grandville objected to our going to college because he thought it might offend the whites. Later he agreed to send Maggie, his daughter, to college. She finished, majoring in mathematics. She moved to South Carolina, married, and had three children. One girl has a Ph.D. in music and one has a master's. They both married physicians. The son took over his father's undertaking business. You know what your grandfather Thomas did since three of us became teachers. My brother Daniel was for a time in the school system but later decided to go into business. Our brother Will attended Tuskegee and became a mason. Uncle John shared all he had for our education because he had no children and never married.

Aunt Mildred

Houston Brummit:

My mother had told me that her uncles Grandville and John had a painting business in Talladega. But when the whites decided that they had earned too much money, her uncles were forced to close their business and their bank accounts were seized.

Every fall, Grandfather Thomas would send my mother a bushel of raw peanuts, which she would roast in our kitchen oven until they were edible. He had been able to keep the farm work going with the help of Lena, his second wife, and Gaines, his son by that marriage. Mother and I had visited Talladega and the McLeod homestead one summer, about 1935, when I was seven or eight. In that part of the rural South, the mode of transportation was generally mule and buggy. The barns were old wooden structures whose sun- and rain-bleached boards were dark gray and warping away from their frames, unlike the smoothed, probably green timbers seen in Denzel Washington's 2007 film *The Great Debaters.*

The main house sat on the top of a small hill with a road leading out toward the town of Wilsonville. I remember a four-room house with a kitchen and beautiful dark, I assume walnut, floors and ceilings. I had never seen wooden ceilings before and perceived them as strange, so I would spend time gazing up at them.

Instead of a modern bathroom with indoor plumbing which I had expected, there was a forbidding outhouse with bottomless pits where I imagined all sorts of weird, odious creatures squirmed. Outside of the house were fenced-off areas with chickens, geese, ducks, pigs, mules, and cows. My biggest disappointment was the milk. The cows usually produced fresh, rich milk, but they had been eating bitter grass that summer, so while I was there, the resulting milk was bitter.

Part III

The Lure of Talladega

Houston Brummit:

The attraction of oral history is in its personalized truth. Eyewitnesses narrate events according to their own perspectives. History is what they say it is. I am aware that the timeline in the life of William H. Brummit is, at parts, sketchy, even inaccurate. Lost memory is the most likely culprit in explaining why "holes" occur in the telling of his story. On the other hand, oral history participants may be guilty of embellished memory that can augment a reality to the point that factual events are unrecognizable. Self censorship also plays a significant role. The participants may deliberately withhold information to lessen, even avoid, the more unflattering portraits of themselves and others. Sometimes, the truth is hard to face. Despite such occurrences, William H. Brummit's life emerges. We are able to create a narrative that is based on research and census data, but the flesh and blood of the man is realized in the most fundamental events that mark the human experience: birth, rites of passage, marriage, and death. The mundane and the marvelous happen in between.

So what happened after 1889 when twenty-year old William left the farm? We know that he sought more formal education and went to a two-year junior high school. His pursuit of education, however, may not have been his idea alone. The influence of William's mother, Judy Fargason, cannot be ignored. Judy was aware of the existence of an "outside" child that her husband, Young, had sired. Knowing that the mother had plans to have her child educated in Talladega, Judy was determined that she would not be outdone and demanded that the same be done for William—but it wasn't. I can only speculate that William's father had the final word and insisted that his first and oldest child stay in Camp Hill to work the farm. But years of pent-up resentment may have been the catalyst that made William throw his hoe aside and go to Talladega.

Alabama's Talladega may have been one of the more progressive, small-town Southern communities during Reconstruction. Throughout the South, oppressive laws had regulated every aspect of a slave's life, including education. "In the Matter of Color— Race & The American Legal Process: The Colonial Period," A. Leon Higginbotham Jr., historian, legal scholar, and federal court judge, discusses how Georgia law in the mid-1750s "resolved" the education issue:

> Particularly revealing was the prohibition against teaching a slave to read or write—an act that elicited a penalty of fifteen pounds sterling. Previously, the trustees had not only permitted the education of Georgia slaves, but had affirmatively financed a catechist for their instruction. Now, the financial penalty for teaching a slave was 50 percent greater than that for willfully castrating or cutting off the limb of a slave.

It is interesting to note that a few slaves still managed to learn how to read and write. Pearl's account reveals that Young Brummitt's white half-brother and half-sister "wanted to teach him," even though Young's father and slave owner "didn't want it done."

With the close of the Civil War, freedmen and newly freed slaves pushed to establish schools. One such school was Talladega College, begun as a small, private, liberal arts institution on November 20, 1865, by former slaves William Savery and Thomas Terrant. Aided by the Northern general, Wagner Swayne, Savery and Terrant constructed a one-room schoolhouse that immediately exceeded capacity because blacks were so desperate to be educated. Realizing the need for expansion, General Swayne successfully persuaded the American Missionary Association to purchase the nearby Baptist Academy (about to be sold due to a mortgage default), along with its twenty acres. Grateful to Swayne, Baptist Academy was renamed Swayne School in honor of the general. In November 1867, the judge of probate of Talladega County issued a charter for Swayne School to be renamed Talladega College. The college is now situated on fifty acres on the outskirts of the city. It is the oldest historically black college in Alabama.

Among private liberal arts colleges today, Talladega College is ranked first in Alabama and listed sixty-fourth in the nation by the *Washington Journal.*

Olla Brummit confirmed that my grandfather lived the first twenty or more years of his life on the farm, worked as a farmer, and had no formal education, yet he somehow taught himself to read—or had instruction from his father, a bible reader. At some point, he must have felt a strong need to escape the intellectual vacuum and isolation of rural life for urban vocational goals. To that end, he defied tradition by walking off the farm without his father's permission. William knew that in Talladega he would be able to find work and enter the Talladega school system.

Olla:

The teachers didn't know what grade to assign him because he was a young adult and had no formal education. As a long, tall 6' 3", they put him in the seventh grade. He chose a seat near the door that was close to the books. You see all he wanted to do was read books. His desk was close to the door that led to the hall, and his legs would sprawl out in the aisle. When the teacher came in one day, she said that she didn't know that someone had left the classroom door open. Then she asked, "Brummit, please close the door." Instead of shutting the door soft and easy, he slammed the door shut with his foot and continued reading. When no one said anything and he didn't look up from his reading, the next thing he heard was the teacher's sarcasm: "Now tell me, Brummit, just how country you are and how uncouth." He was so country and ignorant; he didn't know how to behave in a classroom.

Anyway, he had no academic problems in high school because he was one of the older ones. He took English, all the math, and everything. He generally read while all the other school children were sitting and playing. Since he was one of the oldest ones, he paid no attention to them. When he was in the country, he would read and write everything he could get his hands on.

William said that there was this Negro man who owned a little store on the Talladega College campus where all the students would go to buy their candies and cakes. He didn't have enough sense to take the money he brought from the farm to the school office. He just didn't know what to do with it. Being very friendly with the storeowner, William gave his money to this man to keep in his store. When he needed to purchase supplies and things, he went back to this man, who said he didn't have it but would dwindle it back to him as he got the money. Your grandfather would talk so much about the hardships he had that the man became interested enough to want him to stay and get an education. The man offered him a job because he still owned acres and acres of land down there and promised William that if he helped them out on the farm with the cows and other chores, he wouldn't want for anything. For your grandfather it was, "Oh, no!" He didn't want anything like what he had come from. So the man arranged for him to get another job.

The missionary school had three or four buildings on the college campus, and each one was three or four stories high. There was this big building with "clogs" and "staffs" in the buildings. These buildings had been there for years, and during slavery this was a white boys' school. During Reconstruction, the North took over everything they wanted. They took this school and opened it up for Negroes. That's how they got the American Missionary Association to come and administer the school.

All the teachers at Talladega were white even when I went there, except for one black woman who was teaching for a white teacher. Later, the school administrators hired a black man, Mr. Pinkens. He was one of the first black men to graduate from Yale University. He came from Kansas and walked barefooted to a school in Talladega. He had no clothes, no nothing, just rags, but he wanted to go to school. He was a big black man, big-lipped, but brilliant. The school took him in and educated him. He didn't have a thing, and nobody had given him anything. When he graduated from Yale, he came back South to teach at Talladega. He taught Latin even though it was not his field, proving his intellectual brilliance.

:

Houston Brummit:

In 1891 William completed junior high school and went on to high school, from which he graduated in 1895, at the age of twenty- six.

Olla:

While your grandfather was in Talladega, an older sister he was very close to died. When he got word of her passing, he took all his money and went home. While there, William had heard that the country school needed a teacher and inquired about the position. A Negro man, who "ran" things in the black community, informed someone he reported to of your grandfather's interest. Because your grandfather didn't have a license to teach, the town didn't have to pay him the regular salary. Well, he saved his money with the intention of returning to Talladega.

Part IV

The Three Wives of William H. Brummit

Houston Brummit:

While William taught in the country, it was in the performance of his duties he met Maggie Rainey, a young teacher three years his junior. But the marriage was short-lived. In 1895, at twenty-three years old, Maggie Rainey Brummit died of tuberculosis; William was a widower at twenty-eight. Little was known about his first marriage, but Olla reveals that William was devastated by Maggie's death, and it took him months to recover from his loss.

Olla:

Maggie died the same year he married her. He confessed to me that he really lost his mind because he was so in love with that girl. Both of them had been teaching in a little Alabama town. After her death, William learned to cut hair in his hometown. At that time, very few Negroes went to college, so he had to learn to cut hair. After he got on his feet and didn't know what else to do, he returned to school in Talladega.

Pearl:

I know his first wife was about my height and darker. She taught school, and she was very likeable and friendly right up to the day she died.

Houston Brummit:

Maggie's untimely death may have been the impetus to spur him away from Camp Hill and return to Talladega. There, he attended two years of college for his "normal" college degree, (comparable to an associate degree at a modern-day, junior college). We can assume that during this time he considered the medical profession s a career. Zula, the family historian, reminds us that his mother had family members who were doctors. One can only guess that these relatives implied to him the possibility of his pursuing the medical profession as a career.

If the now-thirty-year-old widower was as distraught about his first wife's passing as Olla has led us to believe, his eventual union with Anna Green may have been a "rebound" marriage. It is probable that he met and married Anna, a Nashville native, in the winter of 1899. Anna, who was ten years younger than William, gave birth to their first child, Katherine, in 1899; Houston Whitelow was born the following year.

In 1900, the same year as his son's birth, William enrolled in Meharry Medical College. He must have felt the strain of his new roles as husband and father. He was supporting his young, growing family on a barber's salary while also trying to save for his education. To exasperate matters, he was pulled in three directions: during the academic year, he was in Nashville, Tennessee, taking classes at Meharry; during the summer, he lived and worked in Birmingham, Alabama, as a barber; and with the free time he had, he visited his family living on the Brummitt farm in Camp Hill. Both his children, in fact, were born at Camp Hill, perhaps to an absentee father. In June 1904, at age 34, he graduated from Meharry.

Olla:

When he graduated from Meharry, his family didn't want him to stay in Nashville and leave his wife and the children on the farm for fear that if he left them, he wouldn't come back. In their favor was his intention to return to Alabama. A white doctor had met William at the medical school and invited him to visit his office and his library. When he was about to graduate, that doctor invited him to come to Birmingham to set up his practice, but William never went there.

Houston Brummit:

In 1905, he secured some form of medical internship and studied for, and passed, the Alabama state medical license. Once these feats were accomplished, he returned to Talladega.

But in 1910 tragedy again struck William when Anna, at age 30, succumbed to tuberculosis. In a way, her death was his reprieve; he was freed from marital responsibilities, but not parental. At the time of their mother's death, Katherine was ten and Houston Whitelow, nine. Both were accustomed to living on the Brummitt farm, but now with William living a more prosperous life, he could afford to hire help to care for his children in his own home. From 1910 until 1914 he was a wealthy widower and perhaps Talladega's most eligible bachelor. While another man might have wanted an expedient marriage in order to supply a mother for motherless children, William, most likely, felt trepidation. In his newfound freedom, William H. Brummit, M.D., had his pick of eligible women in and around Talladega and, to employ contemporary usage, Dr. Brummit "played the field."

Anna Green Brummit,
second wife of William H. Brummit and paternal grandmother
of Houston Brummit

According to research by my step-nephew, Dr. Forrester Lee, my grandmother had died so early in her life that the younger Green family descendants were unaware of her existence. She is listed in the 1880 Census of Robertson County, Tennessee, just north of Nashville. Her father was said to be the son of Joseph A. Green, a white businessman, and Nicey, a slave on the Cheatham Plantation near the Wessyngton (Washington) Plantation. It is possible, however, that Anna's real grandfather was Benjamin Simms, a white slave overseer hired by George Washington and his brother, Joseph, to run their plantation, the largest tobacco farm in Tennessee. John Baker's *The Washingtons of Wessyngton Plantation*, which was published in 2009, diligently combs the account books, personal interviews, photographs, and other ephemera detailing the various Wessyngton descendants, among them, the Greens.

Pearl:

Anna was a pretty woman, very fair-skinned and didn't do anything about trying to pass. She was comfortable in just being herself. She had long hair down to the middle of her back. She was a friendly thing and just as nice to us as she could be. We were kids, and she used to put her clothes on me and let me wear some of her nice ones. Eventually, she died in mama's house.

Zula:

I don't remember much about William, my oldest brother because he was not at home enough for me to know him until he became a doctor. While he was attending Meharry, he married Anna Green. They had two children: Katherine, also known as Willie or Bill, and Houston. Anna became ill, and he brought his family to Camp Hill from Birmingham, Alabama. Anna had tuberculosis and didn't live very long. She is buried in Camp Hill, maybe in the Brummitt Cemetery up at the school. Dr. Brummit left Willie and Houston with us until he could establish a practice in Talladega. He then came and got his children and hired a housekeeper to look after them.

Houston Brummit:

When I interviewed Olla Brummit, my grandfather's third wife, she was nearly eighty years old. Her memory was intact, particularly in narrating her courtship and early-married life.

What was it about the naïve, unremarkable Olla Orr that prompted him to target her as the third (and last) Mrs. Brummit? By 1913, Olla had completed two years of normal college and one year of practice teaching. That summer when William began his intense pursuit and courtship of the twenty-ish Olla, she was quite reluctant about getting involved with a twice-widowed, worldly, middle-aged man; however, at forty-four, he knew what he wanted, and what he wanted was a young, robust, malleable partner to manage his pharmacy and to assist him in other business affairs. By January 1914, they were married.

Olla:

At thirty-seven, William Brummit returned to Talladega as a physician after graduating medical school; I was in the eighth grade. While he was our family doctor, I really didn't have any medical troubles. We all knew him because he worked around in the neighborhood and he was outstanding. Everyone was so proud of him, but I thought nothing about him until after I had taught a year and I had come home for a vacation.

He was frequently around your mother's family, where her aunts came in all the skin colors, with hair down their backs. Like Kate, they were proud and aloof. Well, he had socialized with all those people who were older than I. People were always trying to introduce him, and people from out of town would be waiting for him. They'd come down on summer vacation and board all around town when I was just a teenager and paying no attention to it. There wasn't anyone around that I was interested in except for another fellow, a very handsome young man, and our families knew each other.

It was the first year I was teaching. My girlfriend lived in a large house, and there was a woman staying there who had brought her child from Selma, Alabama, up to Talladega to have Doctor to treat her. People came from all over the state to see Doctor. My girlfriend, Bertha, and I wanted to go to a picnic, and if one of us couldn't go, the other would have a fit and vice versa. So this woman and her child were staying at Bert's, and that Sunday Bert and I had been somewhere, and when we got back, I spent the night at her home. The next morning, Bert's mother told me that Dr. Brummit was in the house, but that made no difference since Bert and I were used to traveling between our homes. Bert said, "Wait, I have to do so-and- so, and then I can go home with you."

Dr. William H. Brummit and Olla Orr Brummit, his third wife,
posing outside their home in Talladega

So I sat there on a couch in the hallway, waiting for Bert to get ready. Then Doctor came to see the woman's child, and then he came out and said good morning to me. Being half awake, I said the same to him. Then he asked if I was going home, and Mrs. Allen, Bert's mother, said, "Yeah. Take her home. I can't get any work done around here with her here. You take her home in your automobile." He said to me, "Why don't you get up and go home since you see they don't want you here?" They kept yapping until I finally got up and went with him. When I got to his car, I asked, "What's this?" He said, "My roadster." I said, "Really. I won't touch it."

William was one handsome man, thin and tall, looked like a Cuban, and was just beginning to gray. He was at least twenty years older than me and had this *car*. I had never been in a car before. He drove me home and, in the meantime—he now knew where I was living—he talked about his practice. To me he was just the handsome family doctor running around with these girls. Then he said something about stopping over to see me sometime, and that frightened me to death. There was another doctor in town, a dentist, and Doctor wanted me to come and play whist with him and Flora Terry. I kept backing out. I said no I didn't think so. He just kept after me until finally I said I could make it but couldn't come until another night. Bertha would be there. Then I said yes just to get rid of him.

It was Friday night when parents would come to the school to speak to you about their children. When I realized the conflict, I went over to visit my friend, Joy. That was when I learned that she and Warren Brothers were secretly married. I wrote a note and asked her younger brother to hand-deliver it to Doctor at the drugstore, telling him that I couldn't see him on Friday. So, when George came in, I told him what the note said and how I was out on a limb, and he said, "Are you crazy?" Anyway, that didn't stop William. He tried to see me the next week. So, Bert and I had this "game." I had her wash some of my clothes, and I was going to pay her for what she had done. Then the doorbell rang, and it was Doctor. He said he was going to a convention, a trip of about three or four miles, and he wanted me to go with him. I lied: "No, I can't go because I am helping Bertha do the laundry." I came back into the hall, and he followed me. Then my aunt bellowed, "You take her out of here!" That was how I got pushed off.

I remember William driving along a road where there was a waterfall pouring out of a hill that flowed into a creek. He knew all about these places and said, "Come on. Let's sit in the shade of the waterfalls." We got out, crawled up the hill, and sat down. He began singing to me, "Down by the Old Mill Stream." He had a beautiful tenor voice and used to sing at the college. I never could sing. He kept on singing about how when he first met my papa, and, Lord, it was so romantic, but I still shunned him. You see, he was older and sophisticated, and I didn't know how to cope. Then this woman with the baby needed soft water and the water at Bertha's home was hard. For medical reasons, he had the woman with the child moved to my mother's home because we had soft water and my mother was a practical nurse. It made it easy for him to see the mother and child when he needed to— and see me.

One day, he said he had to make a call and he wanted me to come with him. Bert told me that people said Dr. Brummit had been out with every available girl in town and he put them all down. That got me upset because all of this had to happen. He never told me he would pick me up and put me down. He told me he had been after me all this time and wanted to be with me by himself. I was beginning to feel that having contact with the man and his attitude toward me made me know that he felt differently toward me—the things he would say to me and the way he treated me. But I was still frightened. He had wanted me to go to a convention with him where he was delivering a talk in another town. I had been at home and Bertha's brother had told us what people were saying about Doctor before he came and drove up to our house. He blew the horn and I went down, and he said, "Why aren't you ready?" I said, "I'm not coming." He said, "You're not going? Why? Why aren't you going?" Then I said, "Well, I decided when my good name is at stake, I'm going to protect it." He said, "What are you talking about?" I said, "I've made my statement and I'm gonna stand by it." Then he drove off because he had to hurry home.

After I said that, I went back to the house. I was sitting about and this woman, Miss Boyle, was there, and she didn't know whoI was. I said, "Miss Boyle, I can't talk to my mother and make her understand melike you would understand what I'm talking about." I went on to tell her the story, you know, of what was being said, the words that were coming back and forth to me. Finally, I said, "What position would you take?" She said, "Now you know what this man says to you and how he treats you. From that you ought to know just how it kind of stands." After he spoke at the convention, he came back to my house and said, "Let's go driving. I want to talk to you." So he drove all around, and I told him some of the things that were said to me, and I said that I didn't know what to think. He said we couldn't act on other people's sentiments. Then I said that he had been here all this time and didn't have a steady friend, which is what he wanted and all that. I wanted to be a nurse and wanted to go to Howard University. He said the same thing could be done at the Goodnow Hospital. So we agreed that I could take instructions from the nurses there. I started in September, and the first thing he did was he got in good with the director of nurses' training. That was the way it was, and by the 4th of January 1914, we got married. I was twenty; he was forty-four.

Years after we were married, my mother had been taking care of this wealthy, white elderly lady whose family had many homes; one was in Boston. Mother was always bragging about me, her daughter, who had married this Dr. Brummit. When I visited their home, everyone knew me and I was in another world. One of her nieces came to see her and stayed about three weeks. While this niece was there, she visited friends in Birmingham, and one was the white doctor, a Dr. Wheeler, who had wanted William to come there and handle the Negro part of his clinic. He would have made out quite well in Birmingham. It seemed like he had all of these experiences, and he would discuss these things with me. He was outstanding. Anybody that saw him knew that he was unusual. He was radiant, outspoken, honest, fair, and anyone who knew him, knew him like that.

Your grandfather and I had a good marriage. I used to make him laugh because he was so pleased with having a wife who was healthy. I used to tell him, "Brummit, you've been to bat three times; now you is out. I've got to be the one who's going to stay," and he used to laugh.

Olla Brummit in her later years

Part V

Becoming "Doctor"
in Talladega, Alabama

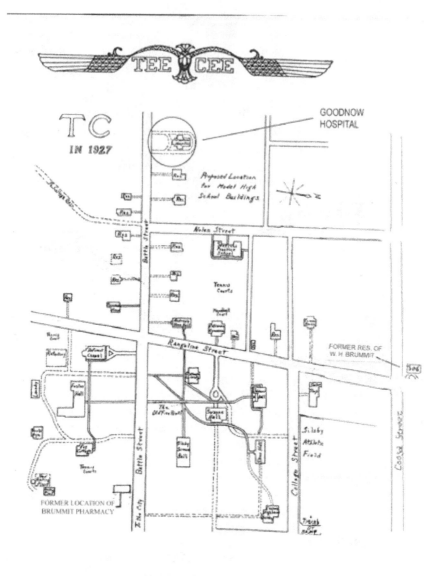

This map of the Talladega College campus shows the location of the Goodnow Hospital, where Dr. Brummit performed surgery, the former location of Dr. Brummit's pharmacy on Battle Street, and the former location of Dr. Brummit's residence on Rangeline Street.

The Goodnow Hospital was constructed on the Talladega College campus in 1909-1910 through a large donation by E. A. Goodnow of Worcester, Massachusetts. It was an active hospital that attracted patients well beyond the campus. The nursing program established there shut down in 1926, two years after the KKK assault of Dr. Brummit. Thereafter, the building served as the college infirmary until 1974. In 1981, it was renovated and turned into a cultural arts center. This photograph of the E. A. Goodnow Hospital came from an undated collection in the Talladega College library.

Current photo of Building & signage

Through the intervention of a close friend and 1947 graduate of Talladega College, Gwendolyn Ball Grissom, contact was made with President Billy C. Hawkins. Upon forwarding my book "Talladega Days" to him, the true origins of the 21-bed hospital built with a surgical pavilion for patients of Dr. William Henry Harrison Brummit were realized. To acknowledge the unsung history of this Negro college, I asked the President and Trustees to place a plaque on the building in memory of the work my grandfather did for the college and community.

3rd from Left, Morris Ware, a Brummit descendant receives the plaque dedication from the Talladega College Board of Trustees in 2013

Updated photographs on this and previous page provided by Morris Ware

Chapter 1

Getting Started

Houston Brummit:

Young Brummitt set a work ethic precedent that my grandfather and his brothers continued. We see that the Brummitt sons worked *for and with* their father on *his* farm, and not for white farmers. By example, Young Brummitt taught his sons to be independent from the limited expectations that whites determined for Negroes and "to be your own boss." Ultimately, his lesson may not have been sincerely imparted, for my grandfather's decision to walk off the farm left the elder Brummitt deprived of a valuable laborer. But William took his father's lesson to heart, and his leaving represents the movement from backbreaking physical farm labor, slave industry, to intellectual challenges associated with the educated, middle class. Even though he rejected farm life, William was overwhelmingly influenced by his father's fierce sense of pride in his insistence to be self-reliant, self-determining, and self-employed in the face of Jim Crow racism. Twenty years of farm discipline and responsibility prepared William for the rigors he would face in his medical education and eventual entrepreneurship.

Zula:

My niece, Sheppie, asked where did William get the idea of becoming a doctor? This is my understanding from something that Pearl told me. Papa had an illegitimate daughter by a woman whose last name was Pulliam. She had a relative in Talladega and she was going to send her daughter up there to Talladega to school. When Mama heard about it, she told Papa if that woman's daughter went off to school, her child was surely going. Evidently, they sent William to Talladega, and I guess it was there he heard of Meharry Medical College in Nashville. Then, too, on Mama's side of the Fargasons there has always been a doctor until now. So, I guess the desire was part of his heritage from Mama, who was a midwife for many years.

Olla:

I also remember William telling me about an incident in Talladega where he'd slipped out the dormitory hall one night and went to town to see some woman and they caught him. When he did it a second time, the school monitors caught him again. When he went to Meharry Medical College to be interviewed for admission, an administrator by the name of Huba had this information on him and asked all kinds of questions. This man told him that he would admit William on the condition that he would behave himself while he was in medical school.

Not having enough money for medical school expenses, William went to work for the Chitam Barbershop in Nashville. It had an all-white clientele, and he would work there Saturdays and Sundays and nights and evenings and go to school. He still kept going out with the girls in town, but in the summers, he'd go back to Birmingham, where all the barbers were Negro, so he could earn more money.

Later, he was hired as a barber in a big, white hotel. During this time while he was employed, he married Anna Green, your grandmother. They had two children, Katherine and Houston. On top of taking care of two children, Anna became sick with tuberculosis. With her illness, almost all his earnings went for her and the children to live on. In order to continue in medical school, he had to work in the barbershops every summer in Birmingham.

There was a prominent family in Birmingham, and he boarded in this older lady's home. This woman could tell he was tired of his wife's mentality, meaning she was not educated. He told me that he was just glad to have someone to open up to, to tell his whole story from beginning to end. He wanted to study medicine, but he had married a woman who was not his academic nor intellectual peer. Also, with her and their children on the Brummitt family farm in Alabama, they were not even together. This lady showed interest in him because he was brilliant. She said it would be a privilege if he could intern at a hospital in Nashville, Tennessee. Since this lady was well thought of by his teachers, they let him do an internship in the hospital where she had connections.

Doctor would always tell this story: When he left Meharry Medical School, he had to return to his father's farm, where his sick wife and his children were. William didn't have a practice because he first had to pass the medical examinations. So, on the farm he stayed there to study until he got ready for the examination. At that time, a *white* Dr. Brummit became interested in William because he was directly out of medical school and knew a lot of new medical information. When the white doctor was going on a call, William would accompany him, and all the way they'd be discussing innovations in medicine. He would always share these things with me.

As a physician, Doctor was always reading to keep up with what was going on throughout the country. In those days, doctors would pour medicines out of a jug. He would have me make special mixtures and prescribe quantities of such and such. In the spring, there would be a medical convention at Tuskegee, and white doctors from everywhere would come down to see some white, very rich man give this medical thing. I think this old man was dead at the time, but every year his son would be there to carry on the tradition.

There's me standing in front of the old hospital. Didn't I tell you that he came there and was anxious to operate? There was this Negro woman's club that saw that Doctor wanted to help the community. So they rented a little train house and fixed it up with beds and things just like a little hospital. The president of the college, whose purpose was to go out and work for the school, became interested in this project and was trying to do things. The college owned these big two-story houses; they opened these houses to him. With the president still interested, he continued to travel and get money for the school. In his travels he would mention the Negro doctor who was doing so much. The family of E. A. Goodnow gave the school money to build a formal hospital in 1909-1910 so that my husband could work. The Goodnow Hospital is still there, but all the good Negro doctors who.

were there are now dead and gone.

Ye Faculty

OFFICERS

Frederick Azel Sumner, B.D., A.M. . . . . *President.*
James Tate Cater, A.M. . . . . *Dean.*
James Putnam O'Brien, D.D. . . . . *Dean Theological Seminary.*
George Nelson Griswold . . . . *Treasurer.*
Annetta Bruce . . . . *Preceptress.*

MUSIC

Kate Waldo Peck, Mus. B.   Lois Hannaford.

ENGLISH

Chas. A. Jaquith, B.D., A.M.   Mrs. Roxie Page Hood
Mrs. Eliza L. Jaquith, A.B.

SCIENCE

Clara May Standish, A.B.   Paul K. Hood, A.M.

LANGUAGES

Mattie May Marsh, A.B.   Mrs. Daisy Rochon Cater

EDUCATION

Dean James T. Cater   Hattie Clark

MATHEMATICS

Homer Milton Taylor, B.S., B.S. in C.E.

SPECIAL LECTURERS

W. H. Brothers, M.D. . . . . *Materia Medica and Obstetrics.*
W. H. Brummit, M.D. . . . . *Anatomy and Physiology.*

HISTORY AND POLITICAL SCIENCE

Edwin C. Silsby, A.M., L.L.D., *Emeritus*   Everard W. Snow, A.B., B.D.

THEOLOGICAL SEMINARY

George W. Andrews, A.M., D.D. . . . . *Emeritus Professor Theology.*
William H. Holloway, D.D. . . . . *Applied Sociology, Church Methods.*
Charles A. Jaquith, A.M., B.D. . . . . *Biblical Literature.*

MISCELLANEOUS

Jubie B. Bragg, B.S. *Director of Athletics.*
Joseph J. Fletcher, A.B. . . . . *Supt. Slater Shop.*
Christine Holmes Sumner, R.N. . . . . *Supt. Goodnow Hospital.*

---

*On the faculty roster page (above), W. H. Brummit, M.D. is listed
as a special lecturer; on the advertisement page (next),*

Hours: 8 to 10; 12 to 1; 2 to 4
Office Phone 503
Residence Phone 7132
Residence, 1416 7th Ave.

Dr. L. U. Goin

PHYSICIAN AND SURGEON
1630 4th Avenue
Rooms 405-406
Masonic Temple Building
Birmingham, Ala.

—WE CREDIT YOU—

Guarantee Tailoring Company, Inc.

Out of the high rent district.

1711 N. 4th Ave. Birmingham, Ala.

"USE WHILE YOU PAY—IT'S THE EASY WAY"

Established 1882

JEWELRY, WATCHES, DIAMONDS,
SILVERWARE, FINE CHINA,
AND BRICA-BAC

R. Heine Jewelry Store

E. H. Jones, B. S., M. D.

PHYSICIAN AND SURGEON

Office—125 WEST BATTLE ST.

Office Phone 327—Resi. Phone 337
Talladega, Ala.

EVERY CENT SPENT IN THE NIF-
TY JIFFY STORE. COUNTS

WOODS BROTHERS

NIFTY JIFFY STORE

Office—Tuxedo Junction
Phone Ensley 1905
Residence—1515 20th Street
Phone Ensley 167

C. Norman Adamson

A. B., M. D.
Office Hours: 8 to 10, 12 to 2, 5 to 8.
Sunday by Appointment
Ensley, Alabama

While in Birmingham, Alabama,
Patronize the

Public Shoe Shine Parlor

306 N. 18th Street

Looking for home comforts? Stop
at the Rush Hotel

316½ N. 18th Street
MR. D. M. RUSH, Prop.

Because we can give you the BEST is
why we ask you to patronize the

New Era Pharmacy

The Leading Colored Drug Store in
the County

DR. W. H. BRUMMIT, Prop.
Telephone 267

One Hundred Thirty-One

Dr. Brummit's new era pharmacy *is advertised. Both pages are reproduced from the Talladega College yearbook between 1919 and 1924.*

Houston Brummit:

At the time it was established, the Goodnow Hospital was the only hospital in Talladega. Whites had to go out of town for inpatient treatment. The first floor had a reception area, fourteen beds, and an equipped dental office. The second floor was equipped with a surgical pavilion and adjacent recovery room. There was an autoclave, intravenous stands, a nurse's station, bathrooms, a sunroom, seven beds, and a sitting room. Without W. H. Brummit as the general surgeon, the surgical pavilion became non-operative. As medical and dental staffs became scarcer, the Goodnow services were diminished; health care became the domain of nurses.

For years, Talladega College had offered courses related to the rudiments of nursing, including classes for women in the community. However, when my grandfather, fresh out of Meharry Medical College, returned to Talladega with his state medical license in 1905, he spearheaded the latest medical practices and ventured into surgery. To accommodate his practice, he stressed the need for Talladega College to have more organized teaching and better health care. In 1906 the college converted two homes on its property into a makeshift hospital, from which Dr. Brummit conducted his practice.

By way of fundraising on the part of the college president, a large sum of money came from E. A. Goodnow of Worcester, Massachusetts. This generous financial contribution enabled the college to construct the twenty-one bed E. A. Goodnow Hospital in 1909-1910 and a surgical arena was provided for Dr. Brummit. With this accomplishment, the training of nurses was instituted in 1910. Dr. Brummit, as lecturer, was essential to the nursing program, with additional teaching support provided by Drs. E. H. Jones and W. H. Brothers.

Files indicate that Goodnow was an active hospital, and that most of the patients were not associated with the college. Between September 1921 and March 1922 about 118 patients were admitted, and nineteen major and eight minor operations were performed.

Years after my Grandfather's death, the Goodnow Hospital was used as an art building in 1980 with no mention of his role in the community. In 2013 a plaque was placed on the building to correct this missing history. Around this same time, upon appraising an assortment of murals which were randomly stored on campus and realizing their worth, the Board of Directors began to exhibit the collection by Hal Woodruff at the Goodnow arts complex on a permanent basis.

Zula:

He used to go to Tuskegee Institute every spring to a clinic to demonstrate new techniques in surgery to the other doctors. Sometimes he would stop by our home to see Mama and Papa.

Olla:

Doctor was a great church worker. He attended Sunday school all of his life. In Talladega, he was a superintendent of the Baptist Sunday School, which hadn't been doing too well even though it was in the college neighborhood. All the people would come because he was a man the people liked. They liked and disliked, you know. He was disliked because he didn't mince words. If you were telling a lie, he'd just say, "That's a lie. You're lying. You know better than that."

Old people with canes would come there and fill up the whole church on Sunday morning at nine o'clock to hear him because   he was under the Sunday school. Alphabet teachers and the girls from college who had never attended the church came down to be teachers at this Sunday school because he was the superintendent. When he gave talks, he was so inspiring that young people would ask him questions and want his opinion, and I would have to stay at the drugstore until he finished. At that time, Frederick Sumner was president of Talladega College; his son was one of the first whites to attend.

Chapter 2

Success in the Hometown

Houston Brummit:

The sacrifice and years invested in his medical education forced William H. Brummit to confront a difficult choice; he chose career over family. Seemingly eager to project himself into the world at large, he soon set out as a physician-entrepreneur, targeting four distinct areas in which to make his mark. First, he developed his private practice. His reputation grew as his natural gifts in diagnosis and surgical procedure put colleagues on notice. Second, he established his own drugstore, the NEW ERA PHARMACY. Besides being acknowledged as a widely respected surgeon, Dr. Brummit was known for his drugstore in the heart of Talladega, where black mothers could freshen up and sit down with their children to enjoy a dish of ice cream after shopping in town— a convenience otherwise unavailable to them in segregated Talladega that forbade blacks to share in the amenities available to whites. He also opened a poolroom that provided a wholesome haven for black men, who otherwise had to settle for the black beer hall or alleys away from the center of town to drink bottled liquor. This venture benefited him two-fold. He not only provided pharmaceutical services, but the pharmacy served as a social oasis for Negroes. In effect, he easily increased his revenues and patient referrals. Third, he acquired strategic real estate properties in both the white and black communities. Fourth, he convinced Talladega College to support his surgical pursuits. Sensing a medical "star" in its midst, Talladega College donated two small houses to accommodate Dr. Brummit's surgical practice. The first house was used for surgery; the second was designated for post- surgical recovery and in-patient care. To address patient recovery, Dr. Brummit understood the need to implement a nurses' training program that would produce a staff of professionally trained nurses to care for recuperating patients. Dr. Brummit's tenacious pursuits in surgery spearheaded Talladega College's campaign to build a more substantial hospital.

The college president sought financial aid and through his efforts, in 1909-1910, the E. A. Goodnow family contributed funds to erect and equip a twenty-one-bed medical facility. With this achievement, the hospital became the reason for developing an accredited nursing program.

Olla:

Young Brummitt was a workingman who put out the work and didn't bother with other things. Neither one of them—the mother nor the father—had an education and both were very independent people. He was concerned with making a living and seeing that the children took care of the farm, which they did. They all had their different duties. Sometimes he grew the cotton, and sometimes he ginned the cotton.

I think the father was off on Sundays when his wife and children went to church. It was far away, and they had to drive to get there. While they were gone, he would kill a few chickens, and when the family returned, they would be excited. Back home they'd cook and eat the chicken. They would tell him they were hungry and wanted something to eat, and he would get the chickens. He always tried to please them.

Young Brummitt wasn't doing too good on the farm, but he wouldn't ask for financial help. When his children asked him for money, he said he had given all of them the "sawdust" they had in their own houses, and he would divide what he had when he died. Young Brummitt was the one who kept working and was still paying for the farm. When William would come over, his father would tell him to do this, that, and the other thing. You see, William was the one who had worked hard on the farm and hadn't been paid for his efforts, so he didn't feel obligated to the farm nor to his father regarding the farm's upkeep. Young Brummitt replied, "I don't need anything, and I can take care of myself." But Uncle Allen said William didn't need the farm. His brothers and sisters tried to waylay him. They said William could give his father what he needed. I told them William lived his way or better than most folks in town. He owned his property and it was paid for. He was the first person in Talladega to own a car. They asked how much money he had and guessed $80,000. I said," No, that ain't true." You see, all of them thought he was rich and that he should hand out money to them.

One day, years later, a man came over to the drugstore and asked for Dr. Brummit. I informed him that he was on a patient call, but he would be back shortly. I just thought the man had to see him for business. I asked, "Who shall I say called?" He said, "Dr. So-and- So *Brummit*." This was the same doctor at Camp Hill who had come up there to see my husband, the black Dr. Brummit. This man and he were cousins, but he came up there especially to see William. I didn't know what he was doing in Talladega. He waited for him, and when your grandfather entered the drugstore, they had the longest discussion. After he was gone, I never saw him again.

Doctor was a lot of fun even though he was very serious. He was a man who could kneel down on the ground and shoot marbles with you. Once he got a call while I was at the drugstore. All the Negro children around the neighborhood had no place to go downtown, and the drugstore was the only place they could go. These kids must have been from some very rural place. This little kinky-haired girl came to the door, walked in, and stood there for a time and looked at him. Finally, she said: "I shoot a good game of marbles." We just fell out laughing. You see, he would meet these children on the street when he was returning from his calls and take time to play with them. The boys would come into the store to see us. They knew I was his wife, and they would have a fine time. If he weren't there, they would come to see me. About this time, this little girl asked me to make William give them back their marbles.

So I said, "What?" She said, "Dr. Brummit took our marbles. We want our marbles. Won't you make him?" So, I had a talk with William about how she came crying to me about the marbles he wouldn't return. I said, "Doctor, those children said you got their marbles." He said, "I ain't got no marbles. What are you talking about? You're coming here saying I got your marbles. I *won* those marbles." He would laugh. Sometimes, he would drive me by to see a group of kids shooting marbles. . In the spring is when they usedto play. He would stop the car and get out there, play with them, win the marbles and go home, leaving the kids crying and all. So they came down to the store and asked me to tell Dr. Brummit to give them their marbles. At that point I realized that playing marbles was like playing pool. You have to call to hit the other marbles like you have to hit a pool ball with another pool ball. I knew he was just brilliant.

Houston Brummit:

In Zula's history of the Brummit family, she seldom mentioned her older sister Eva, and in her biographies, she wrote only three words, "Eva Brummit Hanson," which added the last name of Eva's husband, whom she divorced. It's clear there had been a rift between Eva and Zula. Olla related to me that when Eva visited, they would be sitting down talking, and then the conversation would turn into a heated disagreement. The tension between the two partly resulted from the family's belief that my grandfather tried to run everything because he was rich. She also said that Eva was antagonistic and yet wanted to live in his home.

Chapter 3

Mediator or Activist?

Olla:

Up until and during the First World War, everything was beautiful. It seems after the war, when the soldiers were returning from the army, things just changed. You would see people on the street corners just fussing and fighting. For some reason, they formed an interracial committee, and Doctor was a man they picked to attend their meetings. These people were white, and he was the only Negro. When things would come up, they would have a meeting to decide what position to take or what to do. This lasted for a while, until something else broke out.

There was an incident whereby Doctor was called upon to be something of a mediator or a neutral party to this event. It so happened that Dr. Edward Wren, one of those old established doctors, had one son who married a girl from out of town. The new wife and the son's mother did not get along, an issue which the whole town knew about.

Dr. Wren's son built a home away from his father and was in the process of getting furniture and other things for living in it. The young Wrens had asked George Bridges' wife to come and help them. On this day, the young white wife had gone downtown for something and left Bridges' wife to get the curtains ready with the help of a young Negro woman. There were a couple of Negro men outside of the home who were washing the windows and doing yard work. When the young wife returned, she instructed the young Negro woman to go to her mother-in-law's home, Mrs. Wren's house, and have her send over her blanket. The young woman went over to Mrs. Wren's house for the blanket, which Mrs. Wren said she didn't have and just blew up. She sent the woman back to her daughter-in-law with the message that she was not getting anything and was cursing about the daughter-in-law.

In the meantime, the young woman had been sent out on another errand. Mrs. Wren called up Dr. Wren to tell him that his son's wife had sent a young woman up to her house to sass her out. While the young wife was still away, Dr. Wren came into the house where the young Negro woman was working and proceeded to beat her down with a stick and a whip. He claimed that the young woman had started something between his wife and his son's wife.

The townspeople called Doctor and he went to the meeting. He told them the story that the whole town knew about the feud between the daughter-in-law and the mother and what had happened, and that Dr. Wren's wife had lied. When the whites decided that Dr. Wren was one of the oldest citizens in the community and they couldn't hurt his feelings, Doctor told them to take this interracial thing and go to hell with it and walked out. Mrs. Bridges stopped working for the Wren family, and the Negro men did the same for fear they would be killed.

There were times when someone would come and say, "Dr. Brummit, come and speak for us at such and such a town," or "Dr. Brummit, there's a convention we want you to speak at," and he would always go. One thing he would always say to them was that they had better learn how to conserve their work and take care of themselves.

The Negro farmers grew cotton, and sometimes they would stack it in the warehouses. When the fall came and, in the springtime, the prices would be up and that's when they'd sell it. By that time, the cotton farmer would have to pay for keeping it in the warehouses for so long, and they didn't have the money to pay for storage. This meant they had to charge everything they had to those white people backing them. When they got ready to sell the cotton, the price was up and it didn't belong to them anymore. You see, these folks would have taken it over, and the cotton growers still didn't have anything and would never get their cotton back. Doctor would go to the little country lectures and one of the things that got him angry was that whites told him he was advising niggers in this white man's country. But Doctor would deliver these speeches all over the county at churches and meetings, and the Negroes began to change.

You see, they were trying to change, but that left white men with less money, and they didn't have the cotton to depend on. He'd make those speeches all through the winter, and we'd have a tendency to follow each other and get a little afraid. It got to the place that in the summer the whites would come around and ask, "John, how many bales of cotton you intend to grow this year?" or ask, "If you have any, you want to put them in the warehouse?" But when the Negro man would say, "Doctor's been talking to us, and I'm not going to put my cotton in the warehouse anymore. He told us to sell our cotton." These kinds of things went on, and they had all these things against him. *They couldn't manage the Negro anymore* because he was out there talking to them. I guess we weren't paying attention to them and didn't know what was building up until they attacked him.

Houston Brummit:

Between 1904 to 1924 my grandfather carved out his medical practice in Talladega, only to meet up with the racist forces that would irrevocably thwart his economic momentum and ambitions.

I was told the KKK attacked my grandfather because he was advising colored folk how to take care of themselves and how not overwork themselves. It was also told to me that when he began to expand his office, the noise of hammering and sawing caught the attention of the poor white youths who were setting up preparations for the next Klan march, which always began in front of the pharmacy. They asked the carpenters what was going on. After they learned that Dr. Brummit intended to create more office units on the second floor of the City Hall building, they assumed he was trying to take over the entire City Hall of Talladega. This information was relayed to the Klan office. My grandfather in essence was considered too ambitious and too uppity.

Part VI

Two Black Colleagues, One Black Friend

Brummit and Talladega's Other Negro Doctors

Olla:

In Talladega, there were three Negro doctors: Dr. Brothers, Dr. Jones, and your grandfather. They were running their own offices and they owned their office buildings. Dr. and Mrs. Joy Brothers had three children, two boys and one girl. The girl works in a library in Los Angeles. The older son, a brilliant man, was named for his father, Warren. Young Warren got his master's in mathematics in Minnesota or somewhere up there. I didn't know his other son, George.

Dr. Brothers was a small man, no taller than I am, small and jealous. He was friendly and unfriendly with Brummit because Doctor could get all the practice he wanted. Everyone rated Brummit above Brothers. Brummit was too busy to even stoop to bother about Warren Brothers, who was always undermining him. One of the things that happened to break the camel's back was those people I told you about in the county—like a Dr. Salter—who were using my husband because he could operate on arms and things that Brothers and Jones didn't do.

Some white man owned a big sawmill about ten miles out from town in the county. He had these Negroes working for him. He was sick. They asked Doctor to go out and see him. He went to see him and found that he had appendicitis and that he needed an operation immediately. Since Jim Crow didn't permit black physicians to have white patients, Doctor came back and called the white man's son, who was going to pay for his father's operation. The son called up to find out how much it would cost, and then he called Dr. Salter, the white doctor. At that time, white people didn't have a hospital in Talladega. The only hospital was at the Negro Talladega College. It was the Goodnow Hospital, a two-story building that was for use of the whole college group. Consequently, the white doctors couldn't get patients admitted there unless they were Negro. The whites had to go to Anderson Hospital in Birmingham, which was about sixty miles away.

You see, when Brothers found a patient who needed surgery, he would take him to the white doctor. One day, Brothers saw this white doctor, who was his good friend, drive up to the drugstore and stopped him. Brothers came in and told Dr. Brummit that Dr. Salter was outside and wanted to speak with him. Salter said that the son of the patient wanted him to operate on his father, and he, Salter, wanted your granddad to assist him. Dr. Brummit said to him, "Listen, I had that man's son in here and he told me to bring him in here. I don't have to assist anybody in an operation. That's my patient and I can do my own surgery. I think you're very unfair to try and take him away from me because you think you can. No, I won't assist you. You can take him as your patient because I am Negro and I can do nothing about that, but I'm not going to assist you."

In the meantime, it got so hot with Salter that he called up the sawmill man and explained the situation, and the son called Dr. Brummit and told him to do the operation. So he did, with the *white doctor assisting him* in putting the patient to sleep. The old man went on and got well. These kinds of things were terrible, but they happened. The Negro doctors were jealous because the folks gave Doctor most of their practice.

As I said, Warren Brothers was mediocre. Joy had grown up with me and was a brilliant girl, with her family being able to pay tuition. She quit school when she married Dr. Brothers because she didn't like school. Although we grew up together and had been friends, we were never as friendly as we could have been because of the doctors' feelings toward each other. That kept her from running into my house and me into hers. I never saw her anymore until after Dr. Brothers died. She came here to visit me in Chicago, and we went out to the country. She was telling me the story. It seems he had a stroke and was sick ever so long in a wheelchair.

She said, "Olla, when I think about how limp he was in that wheelchair and how he couldn't do anything himself, it pains me. He couldn't talk, and you had to try and figure out what he was saying. George had also moved to California and had called me to ask how his father was. I didn't know that Warren had rolled up behind me. I told George that he's about worried me to death. I am so sick of him I don't know what to do."

Joy was expressing herself to her son, and when she just looked back, there was Warren with a peculiar expression on his face. She said, "Oh, I was so sorry. I was just provoked and tired and just worn down. I wouldn't have had him to hear me say this for anything in the world." When he died, she joined her children in California.

Dr. Jones was an egotistical kind of fellow. I think he had been very smart in school, but there was something about him that was not trustworthy. He was a pusher, always pushing himself into something he could not do. Like he would go out and get cases he couldn't diagnose. Someone else would have to take the case over and tell him what was wrong with the patient. He was the kind of person who was always trying to put somebody down, and yet he couldn't do the work that the other person could do. So it kept them busy trying to make you think that the other person wasn't all he should be in his work. I knew what he was like when I was there, but beyond the door I didn't know him.

Doctor had become friends with Theodore Kenneth Lawless, "T. K" as we called him. He and I had been classmates in astronomy and civics. He came over from New Orleans, and in the summer T. K. and others would work on a farm until school started up again. He never went back to his home until he finished school. His father was a Congregational minister. In the summer, when Doctor would go on some of his country trips, T. K. would be horsing around the drugstore and just get in the car and go with him. In that way, talking and carrying on, he decided that he would like to study medicine, too.

After Talladega, T.K. went to Germany and France where he met Madame Curie. When he returned to the States and called from New York City, Doctor invited him to revisit Talladega. When he told Doctor, he could not afford such a trip, your grandfather paid his expenses, and he stayed at our house. He had come by some radium in France, and he was telling us about Madame Curie. I'll never forget that we were at the hospital one day, and he had with him this little piece of something about that big. He said it was worth thousands of dollars. He was showing it to Doctor, and we had never seen it before. I didn't know a thing about radium. I went over to reach it and he said, "No. Don't put your hand on it because it can burn you or do something else to you."

T. K. had been there when Doctor had just bought two downtown properties. Doctor was excited over the possibility of constructing a two-story building where he would move the drugstore into the ground-floor rooms and establish medical offices on the second floor. In the other building he was going to create a restaurant. T. K. was trying to advise Doctor not to spend another nickel in Talladega and, instead, to come with him to Chicago. Of course, nothing bad had happened to us then, and Talladega was his home. He reasoned that, "Our women came into town, and there was nowhere for them to sit down. These women came from the country, bringing their babies and children, and you would see them sitting in storefront windows and places like that all over town. They had nowhere to go to rest, or wash up, or anything. I want to make provisions for them. When I get the building fitted up, I'm going to ask the city if they will contribute something toward maintaining it. It would be a rest place for Negroes. They probably won't do it, but I'm still going to ask them."

He and T. K discussed it some more, but Doctor said he was interested in the people around him, his own people. T. K. said he wasn't interested in dying in Talladega, and he told Doctor, "You don't belong here." It was only a few months later that Doctor would be attacked.

Houston Brummit:

According to Martha and Olla Brummit, T. K. Lawless established his practice in Chicago, where he became a dermatologist and a wealthy realtor. Martha spoke of people standing in line to get in to see him. With his wealth and civic authority, he was able to build two twin-tower apartment buildings in a black Chicago community in the 1940s. He died one week before W. H. Brummit. Martha recalled that Dr. Lawless had lost several fingers, probably through his handling of radium.

Houston Brummit:

I was never aware of the conflict between my grandfather and Dr. Brothers. While attending Meharry Medical College, I had the misfortune of having Dr. Brothers eldest son, George Brothers as my professor in a one credit course on ophthalmology. He recognized my family name and subsequently flunked me and required my attendance at Summer school to act as his clinical assistant. I never saw any grades before or after that Summer. It was only when I began writing Talladega Days and learning more about my grandfather's colleagues and their opinion of him that it dawned on me why I was treated that way.

Chapter 2

A Man Called "Mack"

Olla:

After Doctor had been married to me and things had gone well for him, he bought five acres from the college. The banker had asked what did he intend to do with the property, and he said he was going to build a home. Now we already had property: two houses and space for more houses. The new house was in a fine location, but I don't know why he wanted the ground in the center of town.

We lived a step up from the highway. Straight ahead, you could see the red clay mountains. We could see wagons and cars when they passed. Behind and below us was a small valley with no town nearby. The heating plant was in the cellar. The back of the house was built around a huge rock.

When we first constructed our new house, the city refused to pipe water up to it. So he got black construction workers to lay pipe from the road up to the house. That was the first inkling of something being wrong. When they wouldn't give us electricity, he bought a Delco generator, so he had his own electric plant for lighting. I guess we had the best Negro house around. Before the house was completed, people would say they heard we had a beautiful marble bathtub. Many folks, including white ones, would stop by to see our bathroom tiles. To keep up the house, Doctor always kept help. There was a boy to feed the horse and one to take care of the cows because a farm had been part of his life.

The banker asked if he needed any help and to remember that he was there to help us. Doctor said no because he felt he could do with what he had. He said, "Things might be changing around here because we're going to have an older man and a new program for running the city. Since the whites made up the laws and everything, if they had a man like the mayor, who was the head of the aldermen, some people might get on the board and not want me in the downtown buildings."

There were three vacant lots on the same side of the street, across from his white friend who owned a building with a pool hall. He said these vacancies had been there ever since he could remember. At one time it had been a veterinarian hospital for horses. It was thought that the man who owned the properties was a Mr. Wisener. He lived on a large plantation on the other side of town and had his children educated on the plantation. That is where his whole family lived. So, Doctor went over to see Mr. Wisener about buying the vacant lots, and he was told that he would not sell any downtown property to niggers. Doctor told this to his friend McKenzie, who owned the building with the pool hall, and "Mack" decided to intervene in Doctor's name. Your grandfather put up all the money, and the contract was made out to Mack; Wisener thought he was selling his property to a white man.

McKenzie's argument was that he wanted to enlarge one of his buildings. That is how Doctor and McKenzie acquired the property. Without McKenzie, Doctor could not have done it because there was no one else to help him to do it. In the meantime, Doctor had started construction of the buildings and had actually borrowed money from the bank, and all the cash he had was in the bank.

McKenzie's people were very wealthy farmers and had hundreds of acres of land back out there someplace where he made liquor, and he was able to sell his whiskey in Talladega. He was quite a fellow. He had two brothers—all-American roughnecks. When his mother died, his father married again and had two children, a boy and a girl. The girl was sent away to a good college, so you could tell she was educated.

The McKenzie farm had a charity plantation, which was owned by Negroes. Doctor had hunted on it "many an all day long." One-time Doctor took me hunting in the nearby forest, and he took two dogs and a gun. One of the dogs was a pointer, and the other was   a hunting dog that would bring the birds back to you. This white spotted dog stopped like something struck him, with his tail and nose pointed just like that. I thought something was wrong with him. Doctor said, "There's some birds there. You know they won't move if they know the birds are somewhere near, until the huntsman tells them to go." The other one, a shaggy blue gray setter had been trotting on in front. This one stopped too. The first one just stood like a statue. I said, "What do they stop for?" He said, "Well, they are not going to move until I tell them." So finally, he said to the dogs, "Get 'em up." When he said that, the dogs just flew into the underbrush and the birds came out. He shot three quails, and the dogs brought them out. It was the most interesting thing I'd ever seen, but some of it wasn't. He said he could tell that I didn't like seeing the birds getting shot.

This particular plantation even had a cave that the Talladega College used to take the students down to. It was owned by the college, all of it. This McKenzie plantation was on one side of the highway, and the charity plantation was on the other.

A black man, John Terry, and McKenzie had grown up together and were good friends. Terry had two sons and a daughter named Pearl. She never would go to school, was around all day, and dropped out after grammar school. Since making whiskey was illegal, the sheriff always went after McKenzie, but couldn't find him because he was hiding out in Terry's home. They looked for him everywhere but across the road. While he was in the house, Terry found out that Pearl, his daughter, was pregnant, and he was ready to kill McKenzie. Anyway, McKenzie got the girl out of town to Anderson, where somebody there took care of her. This made Terry so mad he got the police department to swear out a warrant to arrest him. So at one point you had the sheriff wanting him on two counts: his liquor and Pearl. By this time everybody knew about Pearl and McKenzie, because Terry had talked about them all over Talladega. While the whites were really mad at McKenzie, he and Doctor had been together hunting in the mountains during the bird season. Other whites often joined them in the hunt.

But Pearl got sick and McKenzie wanted to bring her back. There was a Negro woman who lived in the mountains somewhere and kind of promised that she would get her back. The mountains had always been a place where they could get girls out of town. McKenzie wanted Doctor to see her because Pearl had medical problems and he wanted her to have medical attention. She gave birth to a girl. This was when Terry had a warrant sworn out against Mack. The whites were bothered not so much that he had been carrying on with a Negro woman as they were mad at him for operating an illegal whiskey still.

The court called in Doctor because he had delivered the baby. When I asked what the court had said to him, he said, "Nothing. They asked me what I did medically for McKenzie and I told them. I did not want to get into any of his personal business. I told the judge that what went on between my patient and me was confidential. I don't go out and tell the community. Patients would not like for their physicians to tell everyone what went on in their family and I practice on the same premise."

In years to come, Terry left Talladega and moved to Illinois where he felt he wouldn't be bothered. McKenzie couldn't marry Pearl because the laws of the South wouldn't allow it. So he built her a large cobblestone house back on the plantation. He once came into the drugstore and told me that he had three children by Pearl. He would come in and buy anything he wanted for his family. He often said he was going to move north to Pennsylvania or somewhere so they could get married. She was the only person in his life, and   he was in love. He had twenty-five Negro workers and twenty-five poor whites working for him. They were farmers and each family had a farm. They grew strawberries and things. They would crate and sell them, and the first strawberries they got, they would always bring them to me. Fresh strawberries. I always broke out in a rash, but I can eat them now.

With the last child they had, Pearl got sick, and one Sunday, Doctor got a call to come out and see her. I went out with him, and he came out and said she didn't seem well that morning. So he said to McKenzie, "I don't know what it is, but she should go into the hospital." McKenzie said, "All right, Doctor, she can go right now." Mack went into the house, and when he came out, he had her in his arms just like a baby. He took her in his own car and drove in to the hospital with us. In the hospital Doctor surmised that not only was she sick but she was crying because she was there alone away from her family and everybody. I just wanted to caress her awhile.

Part VII

The Problematic W. H. Brummit Family

Chapter 1

An Overview, as given by Josephine Burton

The following is from a 1973 interview with Josephine Burton, who was a drugstore clerk and aide to W. H. Brummit:

Josephine:

I started to work for the Brummits around 1916, when I was twenty-two or twenty-three. I was there until 1923. I had worked in the country, teaching in a little country school. We'd go into town and there was this drugstore that was a place where colored people could visit and rest or relax because we couldn't go to the white places and there was no place else to go. That was where I met them, Dr. Brummit and Olla. We became friendly, and then I realized that I couldn't continue the schoolwork. The man I was boarding with, a Mr. Drayton, came into town and said I might have to go home because things weren't so good there and my parents were alone. He also advised me to visit with the Brummits since I wasn't going home that summer. When it came time for me to go back to school, Olla and Doctor asked me if I would come and work for them. So I did. I left for work in the morning and didn't get back home until the night. We got along well.

Dr. Brummit was very pleasant, as were the working conditions in the drugstore. The people who came there were friendly, and the boys from the college would come down because that was their place to congregate. They would have what we'd call "Bobby shop" arguments, and it was very congenial. He was very friendly with the boys and the men. Girls would come around, but they didn't, as we called it, "hang around." Instead, they would go uptown and go shopping and then come back for a soda. A few that stopped were friendly and we would carry on general conversation.

I did get the idea that he had a conflict over Talladega College when he was in school. He said that when he went to Meharry to study medicine he was determined to come back in town to show them that he could make good. What I mean was that Talladega was segregated, as it was in the South. So he rented a store in the city building for a pharmacy because he didn't want to send his prescriptions to the white drugstore. Above his pharmacy was the city hall. He wanted a place where Negroes could congregate and trade Negro things. The [colored] people would go to the white pharmacies for cosmetics and then come back to us for a soda and ask for a glass of water. We always knew what drugstore they went to because there were four, and we were the fourth. Each one had a different colored prescription paper, so we could tell what place they had been to. That was why he had his own pharmacy and filled his own prescriptions.

I knew there were conflicts between them, mostly between Houston and Katherine with Dr. Brummit. I worked for them and lived with them. We got along well, but there was the friction in the family that used to worry me. I continued to work with them and live with them for about six years. It was mostly family misunderstanding all around, and we would get this feeling that Katherine and Houston didn't like me and nothing I did could please them.

I always liked Katherine, but she had a dislike for me, which never threw me off. Sometimes she was as nice as she could be until she had her boyfriends. Dr. Brummit objected to her going with the boys because he wanted her to finish school. He felt that she was losing too much time because she would fail and fail and fail. Katherine had a hard time getting through school.

Houston Brummit:

Aunt Katherine explained to me she failed her classes because she "didn't have the photographic memory that Brother and Papa had."

Josephine:

At fifteen to sixteen, Katherine was at the age when her father and stepmother didn't want her to be with boys. They wanted her to spend more time with them, but Olla and she did not get along, period. The thing about it was that Katherine would sleep with boys when her parents weren't home, and she felt her father just objected to everything she did. I think there may have been outside help— people telling her that Olla wasn't nice, but Olla was a nice person. They gave her everything she wanted and needed. They dressed her beautifully, with fine beautiful clothes. Everyone called her Willie. She didn't get the Katherine part until she left home and she insisted that it be spelled with a *K* instead of a *C*. She had always liked to be called Willie because it was like her father's first name. We also called her Bill.

Things began to leak out, and she felt that *I* was carrying news about her going with the boys to her father and mother. But there was a boy, a guard, who used to take care of the horses and cows, and *he* was the one carrying the news. Willie always thought it was me. In the fall of 1923, I married and was out of contact with her. Years later, I knew of Katherine going to school in Cincinnati and then Wilberforce University in Ohio; she graduated in 1927. When I migrated to New Jersey, I guessed along and found out where she was in New York; I contacted her, and we became good friends. I had her keys, and I could go over there if I wanted to. She showed me her will, where her money was and then I went over one time and all at once, she just brushed me right off. She told me she wanted her keys and informed me that she had moved her money.

Chapter 2

Katherine: An Enigmatic Daughter

Emily:

The Brummit family was very respected. Katherine used to often remark that when she'd leave home and walk downtown to where Doctor had the drugstore, she had to be careful not to overlook a single person on the street. It was, "Good morning, Good morning, Good morning, Good morning, Good morning," on both sides of the street. [*Laughter.*] She couldn't miss anybody.

Katherine just loved her daddy. She was crazy about him. I remember once he and Uncle Allen were wrestling. You know how boys will do. Allen threw her daddy down. She jumped up, hollered, ran out of the house, and just had a fit. "He's throwing my daddy down!" This adoration of her father went on between them until he was married his third and last time. That's when the friction started. Before then, after their mother had passed, Katherine and your dad had a father who stayed settled—and single—for a long time. She was like the First Lady to her father. His marriage to Olla was the barrier that came between them.

Olla:

Katherine and Houston didn't have the same temperaments. When Katherine wasn't around, Houston's actions were sweet. He'd get along with anybody. She was the one that kept him stirred up all the time. After he left home, he worked around pool halls. He returned to Talladega, and anything that happened she would just make a big scene out of it, screaming and yelling about anything. If you tried to have a conversation with her, you would be cursed out; maybe you said something that hurt her. And then you would try to stay out of it.

Houston came to me once and asked, "What's going on with Sister? What's wrong?" I said, "What do you mean?" He said, "She gets sick, and my father pays her no attention." I said, "What kind of sickness is she talking about?" He said, "She says so and so and so and so." So, it dawned upon me and I said, "Yeah, she was in the hospital last month, and the hospital didn't know where to find us." I said, "Houston, she has trouble with her menstruation, and then she raises hell when anybody comes around."

When I went to school, my parents wouldn't allow me to attend the public schools, and although I was in a private school, my family had problems paying the bill on time. Consequently, I wasn't always promoted to the next grade at the end of the year. Then I came to this home where these children had everything and Katherine "stuck me up." She could have had anything she wanted. Her father told me about their dispositions and said he took care of their personal needs and I was not to bother myself about them. So, I didn't. Houston used to always get into some kind of squabble with his father because he listened to his sister. They were very bright when they went to school, and they were good-looking kids.

Once, Katherine came in with a new history book or something, and I said to her, "Did you get a new history book?" She said, "Yeah." She said she had to get all the books they needed so they could learn. Until the day Houston died, he didn't know anything about what his monthly tuition payments were because all they did was go there and the school would send Doctor the bill. But in my experiences, I always had to know what my costs were, so I would say to her, "What did it cost?" She would say, "I don't know." I would ask, "You don't know what the book costs?" She said, "Why should I?" I said, "Why didn't you ask?" She said, "Why should I ask? Papa's gotta pay for it anyhow." You see she had that kind of attitude. "Yes," I said. "That's true, but we've got a right to be concerned about what your father is buying and knowing what he is paying for." Well, she didn't have to. She just didn't ask. They both didn't ask.

It was those kinds of things turning up all the time that Katherine could never understand. She'd fuss and fight with Doctor, curse him, and call him a son of a bitch anytime. She always said that she swore the way she did because her father swore the way he did, and she was reared around him. Still she was very fond of him and they were very close.

She was always emotionally contrary. There was this brilliant Derby man from New Orleans whom she was interested in until they fell out when she insisted on going about her business and talked about graduating. It was a one-sided relationship because he was chasing after her and she somehow or another didn't want to marry him. I think she simply didn't have enough sense to marry the guy; that's the way I figured it out. She let him get away, and I don't think he wanted to go, but she chased him away.

Although Willie was a beautiful girl, her attitude was often contrary to her physical appearance. It wasn't because Willie didn't have things because she could have had anything. There's that one picture you have of her sitting on that bench, and she looks like she's angry. That was one of her ugly moods. Nobody knew why.

She could put on the best dress she could find, and she could have had anything in the stores. I know because I would bring things from Talladega. I could even go to Birmingham, shop in the biggest store there, buy anything, and say, "Charge it to Dr. Brummit," and there would be no questions asked. But once she got mad, she would spite me and wouldn't want anything. I remember that I went to the store and bought a beautiful red suit, just her size. I bought this suit for her, and at that time I was slim and she was tall but we could wear the same clothes. So I would try on something to fit her and take it to her, and she wouldn't want it. "What did you get this for? I don't want it." When she had something fixed on her mind, she would harp on it. Her father would ignore her in order not to fuss.

His revenge would be when she said she wanted a party for her graduation. He would say that he was not going to give her a thing for the party and he was not buying her a thing. They would have a big fuss and she would criticize him. Then he would again say he was not buying anything for her party.

I would often witness their arguments. He would tell me if she wanted something, she would have to respect him. All the way downtown, I had tried to convince him that he had to buy her a dress for her graduation. While he said she would have to listen to him, I tried to tell him that she was just too hardheaded to know that, and he had to buy something. At this particular time, I told the woman in the shop that my daughter was going to have a party for her graduation, and I wanted dresses for her. I had the woman in the shop pack up three dresses and deliver them to the drugstore by noon. She could try them on, choose the one she wanted, and I could take the others back.

So I returned home, took the store wraps off the dresses, and when Katherine came in I said, "Girl, I put some boxes in your room with some dresses so you can try on the one you want." There were two shades of blue and a beautiful red dress with an overskirt of red net with little black velvet bow ties. It was a beautiful dress. "Which one will you take?" her father asked. She took the red one. She was all smiles. "Listen and sit down," he said. "I knew you were going to take the red one." That was the devil in him. He was a big tease.

That quickly, her attitude changed, and she said, "I thought Mother was so pleased at me having that dress because she knew it was the *cheapest* of them and kept saying it looked so good on me."

It made him so mad that he said, "You can take these dresses back." And to her he said that he didn't care because she had made him so mad. Right away, she had picked on me. I said, "Now, you take the dress you want, and I'll take the other two back." She took the red dress. All of her friends that she went to the party with said she looked like a doll. But she had been just that quick to insult me. Neither he nor I told her the prices of the dresses, but he said, "Those dresses can go to hell. I ain't going to be bothered with you."

Houston Brummit:

My mother described the same instance when Aunt Katherine graduated from high school. Apparently, she was the only one who did not have a bouquet of flowers. So, all of her classmates gave her a rose and they made her a bouquet. Aunt Katherine herself told me that when she graduated from junior high school, she had wanted a dress, "but Papa gave me a horse."

Katherine Brummit as a Southern Belle

<u>*Joint Interview: Aunt Pearl and Cousin Emily*</u>

Pearl:

I know what brought about the friction between Katherine and her father and Katherine and her stepmother. It was that she was a young missy, and like a whole lot of young girls, they resent their fathers bringing in another woman between them. Then too, Olla wasn't the type that would create an atmosphere of love between them. Some stepmothers bring in this love to where the children are just as comfortable with them as they could be with someone else—maybe not as much as with their own mother—but this wasn't the case [with Olla]. That's where all the friction came, all the hating and the dislike. That was the basis.

Emily:

Willie was the type of person that never got along well with anybody because she would flare up and tell them off. Madeline, a friend of mine, said Katherine didn't get along with any of the girls at school. In a way, she sort of fitted into this "thing" in Doctor's home— even *before* Olla married her father. So by the time Olla did arrived, they were both ready for the duel of the century.

Pearl:

There was a problem between her and Olla Brummit. She couldn't accept her as a mother. I remember her screaming, *"Who are you?"* Olla announced, "I'm your mother."

"That's a lie!" shot back Willie. "My mama had blond hair and blue eyes!" She could never understand why her father married Olla. "Who the hell are you, anyway? In what alley did he find you?" Katherine really didn't swear that badly. Not then. But she was the same one who called her father the s. o. b. and that time he ran past and told me. I went over and gave her a little lecture.

I knew there was something wrong with her. One time she had a boyfriend who had given her a diamond ring. She went into his office and saw a woman's coat hanging in his coat closet or somewhere in his office. She came out and had a big fuss with him about it. He wanted to marry her, and she threw the ring at him. There was another man who wanted to marry her. He had met her in Chicago or Detroit. Doctor interviewed him because he wanted to see what he thought. I don't know what the young man told her father, but Doctor said she was grown. He's the doctor that had begged her to marry him and told how he felt as if he were in a confessional. She had all these changes.

Emily:

Katherine stayed with us one summer, the whole summer. And she and I got along very nicely.

Pearl:

Well, we *did* get along very nicely, too. [Laughter] When I was younger, I was "the kicky kind," and I was still kicking, but Katherine was very precise about everything. I remember she had some kind of a dress. I don't remember whether it was an organdy or something else. She told me how the dress had never been washed. I joked and said it isn't because it don't *need* washing. [Laughter] We had those kinds of run-ins. Other than that, it was very pleasant when she stayed down there with us that whole summer. I don't know why she came down.

She was in her teens then. She was very much in love with this fellow named Irving—I don't remember his last name—and truly I think that's the reason why she never did get married. It was on account of Irving, and that might have been the reason why Doctor sent her to the farm to stay with us.

Katherine with a beau

Aunt Eva (left) with a mature Katherine

Katherine in a "mood"

She and I just got along like kids because I never spent too much time with her. That summer was, I guess, the longest time we ever spent together, and I was always very fond of her. She would come down there and get a school in Chambers County where she would teach. Now where she went from that school, I don't know.

Emily:

When Katherine was much younger, I remember that she would be very jealous when she was visiting. For instance, if Uncle William made the mistake of calling her "Emily," she would be mad enough to fight. She was jealous of his relationship with me. But other than that, she always thought a great deal of me, especially when she went into the WACs. I have some mementos she sent me. She sent me a moneybag with a zipper on it to protect dollar bills and change. Once she sent me a scarf made of parachute stuff. It was hand painted. She also sent me a blessed medal. I don't know whether it was St. Christopher or some other saint, you know. She sent me a picture of her in uniform to our house in Goodwater. Actually, she was just as sweet as she could be. I don't really know what went through her head, but she thought a heap of me and I thought a heap of her.

Houston Brummit:

Aunt Katherine, who remained an avid bridge and tennis player, died September 19, 1972, in the Bronx, New York. Among the mourners at her small funeral were my mother, Cousin Sheppie Spigner Moore, Anna Arnold Hedgeman (the first assistant mayor to Mayor Robert Wagner), and I.

WILBERFORCE UNIVERSITY
WILBERFORCE, OHIO

Class of '27

Normal

Pedagogy Club
Girls Tennis Champion, "26-27"
Secy. of Popularity Contest
Editor of Senior Section, "Forcean"
Sergeant-at-Arms of Gammma Kappa Phi

Katherine Brummit in her 1927 Wilberforce University yearbook

Chapter 3

Houston Whitelow: The Son with a Mind of His Own

Olla:

Your father, Houston, was very bold, handsome, and had a commanding voice. He had a tenor voice, not one of those bass voices. His voice was higher up. It was an interesting voice that if you heard it, you'd stop to listen to what he was going to say. I mean he had book learning. Before he left home, he said he would come back to Talladega and go to school. He had left home and then went on and saved his money. He wanted to be near the city. We were a block from the college campus. At first, he liked to come home because he could do anything he wanted, but soon he wanted to be in the big city. He moved to the men's dormitory on the college campus and was in the same room that his father used to be in when he went to Talladega College.

One night, these boys from some other ball team came to the Talladega College campus. The ball teams would stay at the dormitory and take their meals in the dining hall. At dinnertime, the Talladega baseball team came in, and they came in at any time they wanted for a good cup of coffee. Oh, you know the kind of pranks that kids play and those kinds of things. This night they had some kind of team band, and they had trouble in the dining hall with the boys who lived in the building. There was a student, whose brother was in a higher grade, who had to live in another building across the campus. The boy that lived in this building and some otherboys got into an argument because the kids had tied him up and taken him across the highway to a girl's dormitory and left him down on the stoop. Somebody, I guess one of the girls in the building, went and told the brother what was happening. They all went over to this building to have it out, and by this time somebody had gone down and turned the lights off, so they couldn't see a thing.

Houston wasn't anywhere in this mess because he was up in his bed. But the athletic-minded people and the others were all having their ribbing. Hearing all the racket that was going on in the hallway, he stepped out into the hall in the dark. That was the time when someone pulled out a shotgun or a pistol and shot him in the arm. He was rushed to the hospital.

That night our telephone rang, and it was the hospital calling Doctor to tell him that Houston was in the hospital and he'd been shot. Doctor said to the nurse, "Shot where? How badly is he shot?" And they told him he was shot in the arm. "Did it break a bone or anything?" he asked. "There's no bones broken," the nurse told him. He had been an accidental victim who had been shot in this hazing in the dormitory. He said, "All right. Take care of him and do what is necessary, and I'll see him in the morning."

Katherine was in her bedroom and had been listening. She got up and threw a fit. "Who shot Brother? What happened up there?" Oh, she ranted, she screamed, and she hollered because Papa wouldn't go see about her brother. "No, I'm not gonna see nothing. I'll see him in the morning." She cried, "What about my brother?" They had a big fuss about this, and I wanted to see about Houston too, because I couldn't understand what it was all about. But you see, the hospital explained his condition, and Doctor knew there was nothing he could do. So he just said, "Take care of him, and I'll see him in the morning." In the morning he had breakfast and went to the hospital. It was a flesh wound and the bullet had lodged in the tissue. In a few days, he discharged himself.

But then Houston came down to the first house we were living in. I had forgot we had shotgun holes all in the walls where he and Doctor got tuckered over. Doctor had given him a shotgun for Christmas before we were married. They had got to tussling over the gun and about who had it, and the gun went off. The walls were full of shots where they hit. I said to Doctor, "That's dangerous." That's before I married him and saw all the holes in the wall and he explained to me what happened.

Well, Houston was aching to come out of the hospital and go by our home to get a shotgun. He paraded the campus all day with the shotgun to shoot the boy who shot him. They had to hide the boy and send him home to Selma, Alabama. The college dean came to town to see Doctor and tell him that Houston had a shotgun and was parading the campus. He said Houston was going to shoot the boy, and he wanted Doctor to restrain his son. That's when Doctor got the shotgun away from him. Then Houston left again and went to Cincinnati.

Emily:

It must have been the winter or early spring, maybe 1916 or so, when Houston left home. He ran away from home and came to our house because of the friction and unhappiness in his father's house. It seems that he was being constantly reported by Olla for something, and he was getting whipped by his father because his stepmother had reported something he did or something he didn't do. Of course, Doctor took her word against theirs as to what really happened.

One Sunday night Houston came to the farm and had brought along three or four suits of clothes and all kinds of stuff. It was in the wintertime; he slept in the bedroom where we didn't have a fireplace. He used to tease and say, "Aunt Pearl, I thought you said you didn't have no icebox." He and I used to have a little patch across the road where we grew corn. We used to hoe in the corn, and when Mama called us for dinner, boy, how we would run. He was just so full of life and so happy with us.

I would say he was in his teens when he came to our house, only once. He stayed with us for a while and then he went to Uncle Allen. I wrote Dr. Brummit and told him that Houston was at my house and Dr. Brummit wrote back to me and told me to let him read his letter. It said that Houston Whitelow could come back home, but he didn't want him to stay and live with them. He could stay in the college dormitory. Uncle William didn't want him to stay at my house either because Doctor and my first husband didn't like each other. He then told Houston he could stay at his grandma's home in Camp Hill. So that's where he went until they made the crop, and I don't know where he went when he left there.

Houston Whitelow Brummit's sky pharmacy, *corner of 5th and John Streets, Cincinnati, Ohio (circa 1928)*

Cover Photo: Dr. W. H. Brummit in his NEW ERA PHARMACY (circa 1910)

Houston Brummit:

My mother said that my father was eleven the first time he ran away from his father's home; the second and last time he was thirteen. However, on his final runaway, Olla's impression was that he was sixteen. Aunt Pearl remembered him to be either sixteen or seventeen.

Mother also told me of my father's efforts to win his father's approval through his entrepreneurial spirit. My father started a pharmacy. Cincinnati's SKY'S PHARMACY was a larger and more elaborate endeavor than his father's Talladega drugstore. Like his father's drugstore, SKY'S PHARMACY also had a soda fountain, where my father and Joseph Hurst figured out how to slice a banana four ways and make banana splits with lots of ice cream and syrup for half the price of other ice cream parlors. He opened a successful poolroom and dabbled in real estate with "Uncle Joe," who was able to pass for white. With Uncle Joe in the back seat of my father's big car and my father wearing a chauffeur's cap, they drove around white neighborhoods buying and speculating on properties. It is said that my father was gifted with a photographic memory and was an all- around athlete who excelled in pool, golf, tennis, and basketball.

My father, like my grandfather's first two wives, died of tuberculosis. These three deaths, all premature, can be attributed   to my grandfather, an inadvertent transmitter of *Mycobacterium tuberculosis*, more commonly referred to as TB. This highly contagious disease is frequently manifested by night sweats, weight loss, and coughing—sometimes with bloody sputum and critical illness due to the deterioration of the lungs. It was a major scourge in eighteenth- and nineteenth-century Europe and North America, somewhat akin to the cancers and AIDS epidemics of our time. Presently, TB is a major world health problem, particularly in developing countries.

The tubercle bacillus is transmitted easily enough. Coughing, sneezing, and spitting have been identified as the means by which it travels. William H. Brummit was unaware that he, himself, was a "healthy carrier." This term is used to characterize a person who carries infectious bacteria, does not succumb to its potential lethality, and has the opportunity to pass the contagion on to others. Prior to intensive, scientific investigation whose mission was to identify infectious, yet apparently disease-inured, carriers, society did not acknowledge, or perhaps more accurately, did not *know* to acknowledge the healthy carrier concept. But the case of 'Typhoid Mary' in New York City during the 1900s convinced the general populace and medical community to accept this strange ambiguity: that a deadly bacterium could conceal itself in a "healthy" human body. Typhoid contagion was eventually traced to Mary Mallon, an Irish immigrant and hired cook. William H. Brummit and Mary Mallon, or as she is better known, Typhoid Mary, shared this commonality. Coincidentally, both were born in the same month, in the same year, and nearly on the same day. My grandfather was born September 22, 1869; Mary, on the day after. More importantly, both were responsible for the deaths of others through the transmission of infectious disease. A major difference between them, however, is in their discovery as carriers. The New York City Health Department tenaciously pursued the trail of typhoid victims, which eventually identified Mary as the carrier; William was not even a suspect in the deaths from tuberculosis that took place in his family. And while Typhoid Mary was condemned to lifetime, mandatory quarantine, William, undiagnosed and undetected, was free to spread contagion.

Why, then, did the disease progress at varying rates in Maggie Rainey, Anna Green, and Houston Whitelow when each had intimate contact with William? Maggie died the year she married him, Anna died ten years after her marriage, and Houston Whitelow died at thirty years of age. The simple answer is that they had different immune systems and responded differently to exposure to the TB bacterium, from initial contact to latency period to active manifestation of the disease.

During the nineteenth and twentieth centuries, patients diagnosed with "consumption," the more common reference to tuberculosis at that time, were treated with a combination of bed rest in sanatoria and procedures that collapsed the lung cavities to allow the infected tissues to heal. In 1932, at the age of four, I had tested positive for exposure to tuberculosis. My mother immediately placed me in a "preventorium" for four months. Looking back, I realized that her action saved my life. That is why I find it incomprehensible that my grandfather, the expert diagnostician, did not, at least, administer the most standard of medical treatments to his son. This is a mystery that will haunt me for the rest of my life.

Regrettably, there are no medical records in existence to support my claim that my grandfather was a healthy carrier, and as a physician, I am not making cavalier assumptions about his medical history. In the absence of hard documentation, I must rely on compelling, circumstantial evidence. With no history of tuberculosis in the McLeod family or among any of William H. Brummit's siblings, they are eliminated as carriers. With his first two wives and son succumbing to the disease and all having William as their commonality, he is the most reasonable suspect, albeit, the robust carrier of the germ.

Chapter 4

Olla Orr: The Proverbial Stepmother

Olla:

Katherine was six years younger than me; Houston, I think, was seven. She was just living in the house, don't you see? They were just children in the care of the people who took care of the house. Houston was young, oh, so young. He'd come over to me, don't you know? He was at that age when all kinds of boy books were interesting, and I guess I didn't read all of them. I would listen to him. He left home when he was about sixteen or so. He was such a darling. He called me Mama and followed me around.

Pearl:

I don't know how long they were married, but I do know that she was the type of person that *self* comes first. I don't know if she's that type of person now.

Emily:

That was Olla and has always been her attitude. I know that she said he told her if she managed well, that she would never have anything to worry about. So there must have been quite a bit of money, but I have never heard her say anything about it. She must have been pretty well set because she lives just like she has been living and was able to put Martha through school, and of course, Martha worked, too. But she didn't work until after she finished high school, and then she worked all the time. She was pretty well fixed.

When it comes to "the madam," I have been very closely connected with her, and just like I have told my mother, it would have been very easy for me not to have retained her friendship down through the years.

There were things that she had said to me. One time they were down to my house playing cards, and she got mad at Doctor about something and she threw the deck of cards at his face. Then she turned to me and said, "Emily, you're going crazy one of these days because it's in your blood." I just laughed and ignored it because I figured she wanted to say it to him, but she said it to me instead. So, when I saw her another time, I asked her what was her reason for making that statement? She said it was because my granddaddy's sister had kind of gone off her rocker.

I remember when my first husband was on the road and I used to stay over there a lot, especially over the weekends. One time when I was there in the front bedroom sleeping and Olla was back in the kitchen cooking and Doctor was in the bathroom taking a shower, she all of a sudden screamed at the top of her voice. I jumped up out of the bed, it was dark back there, and he ran out of the bathroom, and when I saw him, he hadn't even taken time to get anything to wrap around him, and she was there screaming, *"You're the meanest man in the world!"*

Now the last time Mama and I went down there, she always talked about the same thing: how proud she was of the relationship between her mother and her husband and how she was able to take care of them so that they didn't have to suffer and have anyone around that was unkind to them. But I knew that if I had allowed myself, I could easily not have been a friend. But I'm not the type of person that holds any grudges, so I just let it go in one ear and out the other and kept right on.

Chapter 5

W. H. Brummit: Master of the House

Houston Brummit:

In the larger world, it seems as if my grandfather saw himself as an authoritative patriarch, a man whose advice and leadership were revered and never challenged. However, in his home, total compliance was only forthcoming from his adoring wife while his children were determined to exert their own personalities. Perhaps unable to see how much like him they were, William might have considered Houston Whitelow and Katherine his opponents, to be strategically reckoned with, rather than strong-willed children who inherited his fierce independence.

Not only was an independent mindset endemic to W. H. Brummit's two children but also an argumentative nature that manifested itself as a dominant characteristic of the Brummit clan. With so many siblings, William, most likely, argued and disagreed with his brothers and sisters, as is the custom with close relatives. It seems, however, that this propensity for disputatiousness carried over into his relationships with his children and, perhaps, younger colleagues.

His position in the family as the eldest, as well as the firstborn son, may have exacerbated his fussy nature. Like his parents, he probably expected deference from his younger brothers and sisters. Given that his understanding of family life was limited to children working on the farm, going to church, and obeying parents, William demanded no less from his own children. Even though he distinguished himself by emerging as the pioneering surgeon of Talladega, in his own home he remained the rustic iconoclast whose pride inhibited him from compromise and, not to mention, backing down from any and all forms of confrontation.

Pearl:

There may have been a domineering attitude on William's part. Like I meant to say, he could have been misunderstood. Like I said in the beginning, if you did something wrong, he would come right out and tell you that you were a damn fool. But, in the meantime, he was going to help you solve whatever problem you had, if you let him.

Now, that's a part I don't understand. I don't know whether there was something that kept him from doing for his own children or whether he just didn't. But I think he might have had pretty tight reins on the cash because he said that he owned so much money in all the years that Olla worked in the drugstore and that everybody was stealing from the drugstore and robbing him blind before she went down there. I think that had something to do with it.

Olla:

As young people, his children couldn't understand that what he wanted most for them was to get an education. Doctor always told them, "I want you to be somebody and I'm able to educate you."

Pearl:

When it came to Katherine, the only thing I know is what I was told, and that was if Doctor went to Birmingham for shopping, he would bring back both Olla and Katherine a gift. I was told that it didn't make any difference what he brought to Olla; Katherine always wanted that because she felt that what he bought for Olla was better than what he bought for her. It was always that kind of friction. I don't suppose he whipped Katherine, but I know he did Houston.

The beatings Houston Whitelow got from his father were very fierce. Doctor used a buggy whip. You see, there were a lot of those boys going to school down there, and they used to work up there because Doctor had horses and farm stuff. It seems like he always wanted his son to be ahead of everything and to do more. That's the reason why he was always reported. The last time I saw Houston was when he came to Chicago just one time, and that was the last time.

Katherine said her father wasn't generous to her. She was always saying that she would ask him for money, and he would give her some, and when she asked for more the next time, he'd say, "What did you do with that 50 cents I gave you last month?" or something like that. So, he wasn't so generous with her. But with us, she would do the chores and what had to be done. I would wash and iron, and she would wash and iron and go over there and give it to the white folks. She and I got along well.

Emily:

Dr. Brummit—Uncle William—was a person that was very moody. The Brummits had a moody type of disposition. Uncle William and I were very close. As to what kind of man he was, he was more like a father to me than he was an uncle. I knew him better than Mama did because she didn't know him that good when she was real small. He was the type of man that he'd go to bat for you 100 percent. If you were wrong, he'd tell you you're wrong. But he would still go to bat for you. Now, he may cut you out, but he ain't gonna let anybody else cut you out. That's the kind of person he was. He would say, "If one member of the family is in trouble, the whole family's in trouble." Whatever came up, he figured they would all have to get together to see to it that the person was taken care of. He took care of me when I was one year old. He took care of my first husband when he was ill, and anytime I called him, he came. My own father couldn't have done any more than he did. I guess I really and truly know him better than any of his sisters and brothers.

Olla:

Both of them were fond of their father, but they would just go off and get mad at him and love him. My mother said that she felt that there was an antagonism between him and his children. She always felt that Katherine was always annoyed with her father. I didn't know what the cause of it was other than the fact that I could see her having this difficult personality. Maybe there was a tremendous cleavage during the years after their mother died when they were reared on the Brummitt farm, so they really didn't know him that well. Then he was, probably by that time, much more caught up in his medical practice.

Houston Brummit:

In 1930, my father, Houston Whitelow, died of tuberculosis at age thirty. I was two years old at the time. My mother, Anne McLeod Lord Brummit, blamed his death on my grandfather. She felt that as a physician, Dr. Brummit should have assisted in—if not completely managed—the treatment of his tubercular son—as he had done for others. My mother was loath to speak of her father-in-law because he had never made any attempts to reach out to her or me before or after my father's premature death.

My mother had an unforgiving disdain toward Doctor and Olla. The sketchy episodes that my mother related to me of my father and the abuse he received at the hands of my grandfather, however, were not altogether in keeping with what Olla, my Aunt Pearl, and Cousin Emily described.

I knew very little about my grandfather except what I could glean from my mother's few caustic mentions of him over the years. My mother spoke seldom about the Brummit family, and when she did, it was to vent her indignation. She said that my father and his sister did not receive the advantages their father could have offered them. She also told me that Dr. Brummit used to horsewhip my father if he didn't open the gate to the Brummit property fast enough. As an adolescent, my father ran away on two occasions to live with his mother's family in

Nashville, Tennessee. He left Dr. Brummit's home for good in his early teens.

William H. Brummit pictured with spaniels, his hunting dogs, in the foreground and his automobile in the background

Part VIII

The Significance of the Color Factor

Houston Brummit:

In Olla's discussion of her in-laws, she had a tendency to disparage those whose physical appearance and skin color were more closely associated with Negroid characteristics. Such disparaging depictions were typical among many Negroes during this time, especially when race mixing was evident. European features were seen, in the eyes of many Negroes, as advantageous and preferable.

When I visited my grandfather and Olla for the first time in 1949, I was received in a small sitting room that had a mantelpiece and two small, framed portraits. Having heard that they had adopted a daughter named Martha, I asked if one of the portraits was hers. Olla answered, "Neither of those is Martha." When I asked what Martha looked like, she said, "Martha has rather Negroid features." Her reply put me on guard for the rest of my visit, somewhat confirming Aunt Katherine and my mother's remarks about Olla's own racial prejudice and insecurities. It also pointed up the complicated racial issues that she and my grandfather had muddled through.

In spite of the racial mixtures in his own family and his marriage to fair-skinned Anna Green, my grandfather seemingly resented having children who, as infants, appeared to be white. His own first name was William Henry Harrison, but he chose not to bestow any part of it to his only son. Instead, the middle name he chose for my father was "Whitelow," which in reverse was "low white." Dr. Brummit's siblings ranged from Negroid to European in features, color, and hair, and it is likely that he had incorporated the Southern white bias against fair-skinned colored people. In this respect, Olla, who would become his third wife, had two pluses: she had brown, not fair skin, and she would not succumb to tuberculosis, as had his first two wives.

What I observed throughout my research was that prejudice was not just a matter of black and white in the larger society. It was also a matter of many shades of brown and the issue of passing for white that characterized the complexities in families, as evident in the sometimes-volatile relationships between members of the interracial Brummit family.

In addition to their oil-and-water personalities, Olla's problems with Katherine might have been exasperated by the color issue: Katherine was fair-skinned with curly hair while Olla had medium brown-skinned and the more tightly curled hair that Negro women would often "straighten." Olla described Katherine as a "beautiful girl" and might well have been jealous of her appearance, especially since there was only a six-year age difference between them.

Olla:

Mr. Tom McLeod—your mother's father and your maternal grandfather—and Doctor were good friends. Tom McLeod married Lavinia, one of Daniel Johnson's oldest daughters. The third son, Gaines, the one with the kinky hair, couldn't learn and was the offspring of McLeod's second marriage. He was just a teenage boy who couldn't do well. Tom's children—Anne, Dan and Mildred— went to live with their grandmother in Talladega, and they never returned to the farm. I first became acquainted with Dan and then Mildred, who was kind of light. Anne, your mother, was darker than Mildred and Dan, but Anne was a beautiful woman.

Daniel Johnson was your mother's grandfather. He was a prominent Negro figure in Talladega. He had five daughters: Lavinia, Nellie, Kate, Della, and Fanny. I know this from my people since everybody knew everybody and their business. Your grandfather had always taken care of their illnesses. Nellie is the one who took care of the Johnson home. Kate was the only one of the sisters who had not left home.

Houston Brummit:

Uncle Gaines, the third son of my maternal grandfather, was educationally deprived, not inherently limited. I personally knew two of his children. His daughter became a proficient executive secretary and an expert on family genealogy. Her brother graduated at the top of his Meharry dental class. Uncle Gaines did have kinky hair, and so did his brothers Will and Daniel; their sisters had curly hair. The result of race mixing is that skin color and hair texture are unpredictable.

My maternal grandmother, Lavinia, had two sons and two daughters, Mildred and Anne. When she died, Aunt Mildred and my mother left their father's plantation to live in the Johnson household to be educated at Talladega College. The shoe money their father, Thomas McLeod, sent to the sisters was used by their maternal aunt, Kate, to buy herself size three shoes. My mother had told me once that she and Aunt Mildred would cry when the September school year started because they wore size six shoes and would have to squeeze their feet into Aunt Kate's old size three shoes.

Mother spoke of her Aunt Kate as being a vain, pretty, and fickle woman who was seeing several beaux at the same time. One was William Walker, who was fair skinned with straight hair. But Kate took so long making up her mind that there was only one man left. He was a dark brown-skinned man named Daniel Bright, who operated a printing machine. She pretended she was happy, but he was the best she could do. Afterwards, they moved to Detroit, settled down, had a very pretty daughter named Lavinia.

Lavinia inherited the dark chocolate coloring of her father. She was smart and always a little plump. When she was of age, she was very much interested in a brown-skinned boy who had a promising future. But her mother prevailed and dug up the son of former beau William Walker. Just like his father, he was fair skinned with straight black hair. So they married but did not live happily ever after because William junior had a temper and had to have things his way. They soon separated but had one son between them. He was nice looking and dark brown-skinned like his mother and Daniel Bright.

Olla:

Fanny Johnson, one of Daniel Johnson's daughters, had married and was living across the town somewhere with her husband. Her family didn't want her to marry this man. He was a tall, light fellow who was an only child. He drank whiskey and never fitted in with anybody. My husband had said his parents gave him everything he wanted, and after he graduated, he didn't do anything. He just began drinking and never stopped.

I had no interest in politics, but there was one time, I guess, when we were permitted to vote. The people at the college were interested, and two or three went downtown to register. These women worked on the campus and two lived in the community, but they were very light, and you would have to look twice to try and make sure that they were Negroes. They could have easily been white. So, someone on the campus sent these women down to register to vote to see if they could get through. You had to go into the courthouse. When they first went in, they almost got through. But in a small town the whites may not know you or have had contact with you, but you have been pointed out, so they know who you are. The pollsters told these ladies that they didn't register niggers.

Houston Whitelow Brummit and Anne Brummit,
parents of the author

Part IX

A Defiant Love Story:

Houston Whitelow and Anne Lord McLeod

Olla:

At that time your mother, Anne, had been going with a young man who wanted to be a doctor. In the meantime, while he was getting ready to attend medical school, Anne and Houston began seeing each other. I don't know how because they never seemed to pay any attention to each other. Then she graduated from Talladega College, went off to teach for one year, and later both she and Houston announced that they were going to get married. With this, her Aunt Nellie was going around telling folks that she didn't want them to marry because Houston was still in school. In fact, Nellie was going around saying that Houston wasn't good enough for her niece, but Doctor was taking the position, "How *dare* you say my son isn't good enough." The Johnsons and the Brummits all had done everything together, had been the best of friends in the world until this thing came up. When Nellie criticized his son, it was like an insult.

Suddenly, one morning, they said that Houston and Anne were leaving to be married. When Houston, accompanied by his sister, got ready to go to the minister, your grandfather said, "I'm not going to that wedding." I said I was going, and he said, "No, you're not going." Katherine had the announcement and intended to go. She had to get out of the house and run down the street the best way she could. All the neighbors knew because Nellie and Doctor were arguing back and forth. I was so hurt because Nellie was my good friend; but I couldn't, you know, go past him and do it. I had to stick with my husband and take his position. That was in 1920 something. Houston and Anne got married in the morning, then caught a train to Cincinnati.

When I was a child, we lived quite a distance from where the Johnson home was, which was nearer to the campus. One afternoon, Miss Nellie came to visit just with me. She said she wanted to see my new home. It seemed that at one time she had wanted to marry a man that they had pointed out to me after I had gotten up in age. But her father didn't want him in his family. That's what was told to me when I was a kid. One day she came up and looked through my house, and then she comes and sits in the living room with tears running down from her eyes. She says, "Olla, I watched all my sisters get married, my nieces grow up, and Houston go off about his business, and I'm still around here." You know I felt like crying for her.

Houston Brummit:

In Cincinnati, my father built our home on Melrose Avenue. He and Uncle Joe brought in a whole slew of fair-skinned colored citizens who worked white, lived in our initially white neighborhood, and socialized black. At the corner of our side of the street was the large brick home of Charles Warren Nash, founder and manufacturer of Nash automobiles. The grounds of his home had a gracious, winding driveway that passed his back porch, led to his three-car garage, and exited to the street. Across the street was the immense limestone home of Maurice Morning, the senior vice president of Supreme Liberty Life Insurance Company. Mr. Morning died the year after my father. The Nash home was sold to Rev. W. Henry Williams, who was black; the Williams were an example of another upwardly striving black family. While we were always aware of the white flight phenomenon when blacks moved into white communities, our neighborhood retained its composition of lawyers, doctors, teachers, postmen and musicians until after World War II.

Earlier in my life, I had never fully appreciated my father's efforts at achieving middle-class respectability, which he accomplished quite remarkably by the age of thirty. One has to wonder why his father did not take pride in this achievement.

Part X

"The Incident"

Doctor's Abduction by the Ku Klux Klan

In 1924 W. H. Brummit, college physician and special lecturer, was brutally beaten by the Ku Klux Klan, and Professor Holloway was warned to leave town. According to Alfred Lawless, several of the younger black teachers seriously considered resigning.

"Talladega College: The First Century," by Maxine D. Jones and Joe M. Richardson
(University Press of Alabama, 1990)

Houston Brummit:

For the South, acculturated to Negro slavery and white supremacy, the slightest hint of racial equality served as a constant reminder of past defeat and attendant economic and political impotence. After the Civil War, a group of Confederate Army veterans organized the Ku Klux Klan in Pulaski, Tennessee, as a social club. They used terrorist tactics to intimidate former slaves and later to restrain Negroes from all social, economic, and political advancement.

With America undergoing agricultural, economic, and political upheavals, the Klan preached rabid hatred for immigrants, Catholics, Jews, and African Americans and often carried out lynching parties in which the victims were beaten and tortured to death. Between 1882 and 1968, of the 4,743 recorded lynching's, 1,297 victims were white and 3,446 were black. The greatest number took place in the South and Midwest, but there were incidents in New Jersey, New York, Pennsylvania, and Ohio as well. Three hundred and forty-seven lynching's were recorded in Alabama.

The whites, and particularly the Ku Klux Klan, were a cross- section of all class levels of America. Whites instigated riots in Florida, Georgia, Oklahoma, Arkansas, and Indiana, and would shoot blacks in the streets and burn down their neighborhoods without police intervening to control the mob. In the early 1920s, Klan membership had surged to three-and-a-half million, and white, racist politicians flourished at a time when Negroes were denied the right to vote. President Woodrow Wilson sided with the racists; during his presidency, he segregated Washington, D.C., and forced the wholesale dismissal of blacks from federal service. The strength of the Klan reached its zenith by 1924 and then began to recede.

The Klan night-assault on my grandfather was reported to police in Talladega on May 9, 1924. Only the *Chicago Defender*, a national black newspaper, covered the story on page 1. With this episode, my grandfather joined the long list of Americans who were targets of a special kind of racial violence—now often referred to by historians as "terrorism"—that had been a part of American history since the late 1700s.

Olla:

We once had all sorts of beautiful things in Alabama. We had a dining room and this and that, and a breakfast room. We had everything—until we had to leave.

After "the incident," Doctor and I must have left within about a month or so. I think it was the first of May, but it went into June. You see, it was something we hadn't expected. Nobody had said anything. We didn't have any confusion with anybody, and the atmosphere had not changed at all. We lived in one of those small towns, you know. We didn't think about not liking someone. We lived on what you might call a "small rise" above the people in the rest of the area. We had flower boxes on this big porch, and when we came out of the house, we always tried to maintain the flower boxes. All the folks down there would see us. If I left laundry hanging out in the backyard and the rain came, they would come up there and bring it in for me, and call and tell me that they had put in my so and so, and then they would tell me what they had done up there that day. They knew everybody who came on the premises.

We were just not accustomed to people being dishonest. Nobody there was. I think in my mother's home we didn't even have a key to the front door. Anyway, this particular night Doctor got home around ten o'clock as usual. Katherine wasn't there. She was living down somewhere else. We had a woman who kept house for us, and she stayed there and did all the cooking and cleaning. She was just an excellent, beautiful character. She had a bedroom and everything in there, and as a rule we never answered the door. The front door usually wasn't locked because we had always felt it wasn't necessary. We slept in twin beds, and the room we had was on the back of the house. We had a guest room and a workroom with all glass windows. My bed was near the door; his bed was on the other side. The telephone was on the table near him in case anybody called and needed something. He never answered the door. If someone rang the bell, there was always somebody else in the house who would see about it.

Well, that night we got the *Birmingham News* home delivery. Houston Whitelow, your Daddy, had sent me a reading lamp that screwed on the back of my bed so I could just turn this light on. For some reason, that night, Doctor had gone in first and had taken the lamp off my bed and put it on his and was lying there reading. When I got in bed, he had the lamp and the paper over there, and I just went and got in bed with him. We were there reading, talking, and carrying on, and the doorbell rang. When the bell rang, he got up and put on his robe and bedroom shoes. Oftentimes, children from the country would come at night and tell Doctor to call someone because their mother was sick, and you would have to come out and listen to what they were telling him. They would sit in the big swing on the porch. Often, there would be four people sitting there; they would be talking to him and then go sit in the swing. But this night, in the dark, I just kept sitting waiting for him to return from the vestibule.

Whenever he had to make a visit of just a few miles, I would go right along with him. I was just sitting on the side of the bed listening, kind of trying to hear because these folks who came usually talked loud and I would hear them from the back. I was trying to find out if it was someone from the country. It was the first time since he had been in that house that he went to the door. I was listening to see if I would go with him, or if it was somewhere around in the community. When I didn't hear anything, I got up and put on a silk robe that was lying on a chair and went up to the front. When I started to call   for him, I noticed that the front door was ajar. I tiptoed because I thought he was on the swing. I wanted to see if I was going to have to get ready to go along—which would mean I would have to get dressed when he came back in. Because I hadn't put my slippers on, I stepped on a piece of glass, and before I knew anything, I had cut my foot. It was then that I looked back and saw that one of the panes had been knocked out of the window and glass was all over the floor.

We had a long drive in front of the house that made a circle in and out. When I got to the door, I could see some cars leaving from the highway down from the house. I knew then that something awful had happened, and I began screaming, and everybody in the town just opened their doors. Doors just flew open, and you could see the lights. Then my neighbor came running across to see what was wrong, and she said, "All right, I know the problem."

I found out later that when he went to the door, he hadn't suspected anything. This time the door happened to be locked from the inside, and they just rammed a gun through the glass. That's why the pane was broken. So, they said, "Open the door!" He was sure there was some mistake. Nobody was after him, and he hadn't had a conflict with anybody, you know, to any degree, and the door was open. When he opened the door, he began with, "What's this all about? What's wrong?" Then somebody hit him with a bat or something and knocked him out. In spite of a blindfold, he was able to figure out the direction of the black hole where they were taking him because he traveled over there on the highway so many times he knew where there was a bridge and how long it took to get to the bridge and all that. They took him down to the college campus and then south on that highway. When he again asked what was this all about, they said, "You're here advising niggers. This is the white man's country, and you're not going to mess it up." They may have said other things, too, but he just didn't want to tell me, even though I wondered what else they said.

Our car was parked in front of the house, and these folks came running across to see what was wrong with me. A young fellow came up, the brother of the woman who kept house for us. In the bedroom we had a pistol on a chest of drawers and a shotgun standing against the wall. He said that if he had known it, he could have gone off with our gun and started shooting. I couldn't shoot a thing. Doctor had tried to teach me target shooting with the little pistol. But the shotgun, I could never hold it right. It would hurt my shoulder. That night I grabbed the gun off the bureau and put it in the car. One of the young men had got up there by the time I was getting in the car to go downtown—I don't know what for, but I didn't know what to do. As we were driving, I told him how someone had come and taken Dr. Brummit away. We couldn't find a policeman anywhere. I drove all around and went to a white drugstore, one that hadn't closed yet—and that's where the whole thing originated. So I waited outside. They *claimed* they didn't know anything or what had happened, like, "What's wrong?" and "Why don't you call the police?" But they knew.

In no time, a group of Negroes in old cars and guns had got together. They took the car away from me and went out to look for him. They figured that they might have taken him fifteen miles out to Chillicothe, Alabama, where over the years Negroes were thrown into that river. Because of those events, it gave them the idea that maybe that's where they had gone. I really didn't know where they were. So, the black folks got in these cars, a whole crew of them, and went off down to Chillicothe. They told me, "Stay in the house, Mrs. Brummit. We'll find him."

Meanwhile, the neighbors and everybody else were coming to the house; it was full of people. Soon, I saw a car turning in the drive; then everybody began shouting, "Policemen! Policemen!" And, of course, there were policemen, who had given the whites time to get away, and they were coming to see if I'd leave. Later, the cavalcade of Negroes came by and reported, "He didn't go into the river, Mrs. Brummit." They scoured that section. There's so much I've forgotten, so much about that terrible night. It seems that the Negroes went on this highway where the Klan had carried him, but nobody knew that the cars they passed were filled with all whites. We learned that the Klan had left him stranded in the woods, about fifteen miles in the opposite direction.

They had his hands tied up, and he said he could tell that there was somebody there who knew him, who evidently came along to make sure he wasn't killed. He could tell by the hum of their conversations that they were blundering along. They beat him with a whip until he fell to the ground and lost consciousness. When they knew he was alive, they got ready to leave him. They were going to leave him in the woods with his hands tied behind his back, naked, without his pajamas and things. One man said, "You're not going to leave him tied up here. Untie his hands."

They untied him and left. He said it took him about four hours or more to clear his head, stand up, and just get to walking into the woods and through the trees until he came to the highway. When he had an idea of where he was, he just kept walking. He was physically shaken by the life-threatening beating he had endured and terrified by the cruel men who participated. He kept walking until he saw a house, a cabin somewhere. He went up to the front door and knocked. He said this little man answered the door and saw that Doctor was a Negro. You see, Doctor was known all over the county because he worked with all the folk. These people didn't have anything but a blanket to throw over him and a little buggy, a wagon or something, in which they put him and started toward our home. Along the way, the cavalcade of Negroes met them coming, and they brought him home. Earlier, the white folks that they had passed coming to town were the same ones who beat him. If they had met, it would have been a terrible riot because if the Negroes had started shooting and the whites had started shooting.

I can't remember all the details except that they beat him, and the whole experience was wrong and humiliating. It was frightening for a man his age with his hands tied behind him, the blindfold, and no clothes. He didn't think what happened to him would happen to a Brummit, the leader of black Talladega, and a man who was just as much a man as any of the other white men.

By this time, the Negroes from across the street, who worked on the plantation owned by Doctor's white friend, McKenzie, came over. I remember there was a Delain who came in and just fell down on his knees and cried, "Doctor, if we had known, this would never have happened." These people felt ashamed and knew that some of the old white doctors were responsible for the vicious attack. One of the persons who came to inquire about my husband's welfare was the bank president and another one of the bankers, Alfred Lawless. Different ones came out, but this one was the one who came early, about daylight and an hour after Doctor came home. Others came; just numbers of people came up there, even a day or so later. Then around town, they had begun saying that it was the Klan. We knew the Klansmen were there because every time they would go on a march, they would break up in front of our store and go up to the college and burn a torch.

The next morning after the attack I came down to open the drugstore. While the whole community was stunned and didn't know what to do, the first person who came in the store was Owens, a little white cracker man. He walked in and came up to me and asked, "What does Dr. Brummit want for that property across the street?" I said, "I don't know." He said, "Well, if he wants to sell it, I'll buy it from him." I said that I would call him. Then he walked right out. That was the first thing that happened that morning after the incident. So I went up there to the John Terry cabin. He had been the former good friend of McKenzie, and I knew that Terry and a wealthy family was behind what had gone on. Even Dr. Salter was in the mob that beat Dr. Brummit.

The white man who was the head of the Alabama Medical Association, a Talladega man who operated out of Montgomery, came up to our house to see Doctor after he heard about everything. He was just dumbfounded. He never thought anything like that happened in Talladega. He was stunned. He came out and hoped that he could be a calming influence, that he could "righten" it the best way he could, especially since the whites who attacked my husband ordered him to get out of town.

This white doctor was the president of the local chapter of the white Alabama Medical Association. That year, Doctor had been chosen to be the president of the Alabama Negro Medical Association. I had known him like I had so many other white people who had lived around town. He was an elderly man who said, "No, this is not going to happen." He said that he had been all over the city to see what the sentiment was. He told Doctor, "No, you're not going to leave here. You are going to stay." Then your grandfather said, "No! I can't stay here. The thing about this is I'm not sure who all these people are. You see, you get something in your head and you just surmise. I get so mad I could kill somebody. It's not worth it. I can't stay here." Doctor said he wouldn't dare stay in Talladega because he would be afraid of this one and the other one, and he couldn't be happy anymore.

PLAN BIG WINTER CRUISE TO WEST INDIES

Chicago Defender

24 PAGES — THE — THIS NEWSPAPER

WORLD'S GREATEST WEEKLY — EVERYBODY READS IT

VOL. XIX. NO. 28.   CHICAGO, ILL., SATURDAY, MAY 16, 1924   PRICE TEN CENTS

High School Principal Is Cleared of Charges

DOCTOR FLOGGED BY MOB

20-Year-Old Girl Held for Death

PRESIDENT ALABAMA MEDICAL ASSN. GIVEN 90 DAYS TO QUIT TOWN

STABBED COMMON-LAW HUSBAND IN BACK AS SEQUEL TO QUARRELS

COLOR LINE BARRED IN WINTER CRUISE TO WEST INDIES ISLANDS

PRINCIPAL IS FREED OF GIRL'S CHARGES

KY. NORMAL HAS FIRST MAY DAY FETE

WEST INDIANS REFUSED SEATS

MOB HALTED BY RAIN OF BULLETS

KILLS WIFE; THEN TAKES OWN LIFE

DANCING SCHOOL AWED BY KILLING

STUDENTS IN REVOLT AT WATERS COLLEGE

Reproduced with permission of the copyright owner. Further reproduction prohibited without permission.

PRESIDENT ALABAMA MEDICAL ASSN. GIVEN 90 DAYS TO QUIT TOWN

Talladega, Ala., May 9.—Respectable white citizens of this city and community have again shown that they are the "best friends of the Negro" by taking Dr. W. H. Brummitt, president of the Alabama Medical association, and one of the leading men of this city, out into the woods and severely flogging him because he practiced on white people, and especially white women. The men were unmasked, are well known and are supposed to express the sentiments of the better class of whites.

According to the story told by the injured doctor, a group of men knocked on his door about 9:30 Wednesday evening of last week and

their claims that they will be protected by the authorities which they help to maintain.

Talladega and vicinity have become notorious for their crimes against our people and up to the present no punishments have been meted out by those who claim to hold the reins of government. Migration is the result. One can ride through the country about here now and see the empty farm houses and cotton fields standing idle, wasting. And railroad stations are crowded with men and women of our Race, looking northward, ever northward, where they can at least have assurance of equality before the law.

Courtesy of the Chicago Defender

Wednesday evening of last week and demanded that he come with them. Tied and blindfolded, he was forced into a waiting automobile, thrown into the bottom of the car and carried into a dense strip of woods, 15 miles from home. Here he was taken from the car, and, after a statement of the charge against him, which was that he had followed a legitimate occupation in his home city, he was beaten almost to insensibility and left in the forest to find his way home as best he could.

For four hours Dr. Brummitt floundered about in the dense wilderness until he came upon a cottage owned by an old farmer who took him in, dressed his wounds and then assisted him to his home. The outrage was reported to the police but no steps have been taken to apprehend the mobbers.

Dr. Brummitt also informed the police that he has been given 90 days in which to close his business and leave the city, simply because white people have more confidence in him as a doctor than they have in physicians and dentists of their own race, and because he refuses to turn down anyone who comes to him as a patient.

White doctors may practice upon men and women of our Race in Talladega, experiment upon them and kill them if necessary, but when an authorized doctor of our group gives a white man or woman the benefit of his skill, he must be flogged and driven from the city.

This action, according to reports, has done more than anything else to stimulate a northern migration movement from this vicinity. Already farmers are packing their possessions and getting rid of those things which they cannot take away with them. They have reasoned that when a man of Dr. Brummitt's standing in the community is flogged on such a flimsy charge as was the case, those of lesser prominence have little if any proofs upon which they may base

ity before the law.

ORDERED OUT

DR. W. H. BRUMMITT

President of the Alabama Medical association, ordered by whites of Talladega to leave town. Two members of Talladega's teaching staff have also been ordered to leave.

Reproduced with permission of the copyright owner. Further reproduction prohibited without permission.

*The Ku Klux Klan was first organized in Alabama in 1867.
William Joseph Simmons, who was born in Talladega County,
became the Imperial Wizard of the revived Klan in the 1920's.*

The more this white doctor pleaded with him, the more my husband said no, and that was that. When the man finally realized that Doctor was determined to go, he began to suggest cities where he could go. One of the places he recommended was Los Angeles because Los Angeles in those days was a long way off. Classmates in Birmingham and Atlanta were asking him to come there. But he had two classmates in Chicago who wanted him to come here to Chicago. I guess that is what led him in this direction. At the same time, the man from Montgomery said while California and Illinois had opportunities, there was no medical board reciprocity between Alabama and Illinois, and at fifty-seven, Doctor would have to study for and take medical boards after all these years.

McKenzie and other whites soon squired Doctor out of Talladega. My mother made some of those arrangements. He had to wait a year before he could take the Illinois medical boards. That meant we had to live on the money we had. In Chicago, he had to buy a new car and medical equipment. We left the car we had with friends. The reason for doing this is that in the 1920s there were very few gasoline stations and highway places to stay between the North and the South for whites and few to none for Negroes between Alabama and Illinois, unless you were traveling from one home to another—no hotels, motels, or other conveniences that black travelers, especially middle-aged ones, could use. A well-dressed black man on a Southern highway was liable to be shot just so a white man could get a free car.

He had a friend in Talladega who was a principal of a city school who was going to look after our businesses while we were out of town. He was going to sell the real estate and the businesses. This school principal, who said he was going to look after things for us, said he sold it to another Negro for—I forgot how much—but we had to get a lawyer to make the buyer finish paying for it. We lost so much.

We sold everything. We had no trouble with that. This man who bought the drugstore had moved his store from Anderson, Alabama, about twenty-five miles away. He bought the contents of the store. I don't know what he did to the building. We never went back. I had been to that school down there, and, at that time, I had a lot of friends from there.

Soon after this thing happened to us, we thought we would never again see the last baby he delivered. And once we left, some of the same white folks went out to McKenzie's house in the country with a posse to do to him what they did to Doctor. Now, you see, being white, Mack had relatives all over town and had ways of getting information. Somebody told him that there was this type of stirring up. So he got all the Negroes on the farm and all the whites to hide in the bushes around there. When the white posse came out there that night, there was such a shooting. One of the men, Doctor said, was a man he thinks came after him that night. Some big man in the posse was shot. So it was like retaliation, a payback on the white community. They were after McKenzie, but Mack had time to prepare. Knowing what had happened to Doctor, the shoot-out was somewhat of a revenge. That man who was shot was never well again.

Houston Brummit:

In the days when there were Pullman sleeping coaches, the Pullman porters who attended these coaches were black and very much accustomed to picking up persons in the middle of the night or early morning hours who were fleeing from vigilante persecution. These victims, who were usually black, would be secreted out of the South and dropped off at safer Northern locations. This was the twentieth century "underground railroad."

Emily:

I lived in Birmingham, and I was going to Miles College at the time. From what I have heard—now I never did hear him say anything about it—but it was rumored here that Doctor was treating a white woman that nobody had been able to help; nobody could do anything for her. Then she sent for Doctor and he went, and this woman was cured of her illness. In order to show her gratitude, it seems she gave him a new carpet. Now, that is what I heard through the grapevine. I do know that he had what you might call an uncanny type of insight when it came to diagnoses. He was really a diagnostician; there's no doubt about it. That's all I know about the incident, and of course, it seems that he was betrayed by one of his fellow physicians. They only had two down there at the time: Brothers and Jones. Brothers was the only one I ever heard anything about. And on that particular night, someone knocked, my uncle went to the door, and they just spirited him right off and beat him. They told him they didn't intend to kill him, but they intended to impress upon his mind that he would keep his so-and-so hands off of white women from then on.

Houston Brummit:

In June 1926, the American Missionary Association (AMA) published an article written by Rev. William Lloyd Imes titled, "A Visit to Talladega College," which re-examined the assault on Dr. Brummit. In the article, the incident is virtually obscured by another discussion, and the fundamentally racist nature of the assault is called into question:

> The influence of Talladega in its community is undoubtedly good. As far as a casual visitor can see, there is no pronounced hostility of the Southern white people in evidence. Even in the regrettable case of the Negro physician beaten by the Ku Klux Klan some time ago, there is no evidence that the affair was wholly on racial grounds; and in spite of many wrongs that intelligent and self-respecting colored folks have to endure in the south, yet it would be far worse but for the fight and help of strong centers of Christian culture like Talladega.

The American Missionary Association waited two years to comment on the assault. That the incident occurred within the AMA's area of operation was certainly a blow to the reputation of the association and functioned as a commentary on its impact on influencing "Christian" behavior. The AMA might have delayed public acknowledgment of the incident because it thought a cooling-down period in Talladega was essential to town "security" and order. Or, more likely, the AMA opted to safeguard the reputation of the white missionaries by concealing their vulnerability, specifically in being able to eradicate Klan activity. Also, the association, most probably, was concerned about the effect of the publicized incident on benefactors. Lastly, the missionaries did not want to, and could not, alienate the power brokers, the white Southerners, the ultimate authority in Talladega.

Part XI

In Transition:
From Alabama to Illinois

Chapter 1

The Chicago Years

Houston Brummit:

After his abduction and assault by the Ku Klux Klan, William H. Brummit was ordered to sell his downtown properties and leave town. Without him, the nursing program at Talladega College hospital collapsed, and patients of both races had to seek competent treatment elsewhere. Instead of resettling in Birmingham, as he had been invited to do, he refused and relocated to Chicago, where he had to adjust downward to a more modest means and position, punishing him with professional oblivion that lasted from 1924 until his death in 1949.

Olla:

When we first came to Chicago, we stayed in a doctor's home. This doctor had just died and left his wife a beautiful home and two sons, and that's where we lived. His wife knew a Mrs. Reddick because she knew everybody. I remember Mrs. Reddick because the doctor's widow had told us about her. You came here and said you were staying with her. You see, in those days, there weren't as many Negroes in Chicago as there are now, but they were of a higher caliber. Back then, the Negroes were initially flourishing. They were all so proud of their homes.

There was a bank there, the Conversion Bank, and my husband's office was in the bank building. In fact, so was Dr. Howard's, who graduated with him. They were prouder of themselves, and they accepted us so completely. They were lovely to us. It was Dr. Howard who met me at the train when I came up. Doctor was already here. It was the South Parkway community, and when your grandfather arrived, it was white, all white. It was kept up well. You saw the first neighborhood we were in when your grandfather died. By that time it was all run down where the Negroes were, and then we moved to South Shore. Whites moved away.

Doctor couldn't work as a physician in Chicago because he hadn't yet taken the Illinois medical examination. In the meantime, he became an assistant to many physicians in this town because if you are alone in your practice, people don't know you. But if you're in the office with another doctor, you can work with him. In this way, Doctor was able to build up a small practice.

Then the lieutenant governor who was in office asked him to come out and speak to some white students. I went with him. Actually, he was being tested for the medical examination. I thought I was so unnecessary and in the way. He met these people at the County Hospital, and Dr. T. K. Lawless and another friend, a Dr. Mahoney, were there. It was going to be an oral examination. They sent in this Negro patient for him to examine. In those days, it had to be a Negro. Doctor had to examine him and tell the observing doctors what was wrong with him. The patient had been instructed not to talk, that is, not to tell him anything. So Doctor came in and went over this man, and when he would ask him something, the man wouldn't answer. He couldn't tell Doctor what was wrong with him. Finally, Doctor said, "Look here, I can't find a damn thing wrong with you." So the patient laughed. Doctor passed the examination.

Many years after we moved to Chicago, McKenzie from Talladega wrote your grandfather a card. Then one day, all of a sudden, somebody rang our doorbell and came up. We lived on the second floor. I opened the door and there stood this woman about my age and my kind of color. I knew I had seen her somewhere, but she was with a young man and a woman. The young couple could have passed for Cubans or something. So I stood there, and she said, "Olla. Don't you know me?" I said, "No. I know I've seen you, though." She said, "I'm Pearl Terry." She was with her daughter and her daughter's husband.

I asked them in and I said, "Well, Pearl, it's been such a long time." We just talked for hours. At that time, the couple was living in the

Roosevelt Housing across the street from Doctor's Chicago office. Pearl had come up to visit this young couple who had one child. The wife was the baby that Doctor had delivered the last time McKenzie had called on him in Talladega. She was here in Chicago going to college and teaching. Her husband was attending Chicago University. McKenzie was still alive, and he had a son. I really didn't know what happened because we had been away from Alabama for some time.

Pearl had said to me that her daughter and son-in-law wanted her to come up here, and when she came, they thought she would stay and take care of their kid, you know, while they would be out running around having a good time. "My son now has extra work at the college and is working on his Ph.D.," she said. "I'm not going to be a nursemaid. I believe in Talladega, too. I'm going back home." So, she went back home. Doctor was enthused about seeing Pearl's daughter because she was the last baby he had delivered in Talladega and he used to wonder whatever had happened to her.

Houston Brummit:

Twenty-three years before I formally interviewed Olla Brummit, I had been advised by my Aunt Katherine to visit my grandfather. He had just been released from a hospital where he had undergone prostate surgery. I stayed in the home of her friend, Mrs. Reddick. She was fascinating to me because she reminded me of my Aunt Mildred and some of Aunt Katherine's friends who could pass for white.

Emily:

When Doctor came to Chicago, people were constantly having him speak. He first joined the Pilgrim Baptist Church, and they were always calling on him to tell his experiences about the incident that occurred down there. But I never did hear him tell the story. Never did. Whatever I heard was while I was in school. That's when they left Talladega and went to Florida. I think an aunt has some people there. Then he left and came to Chicago. Now, why he chose this place—I know he would go around to different doctors' offices, Dr. Howard and several others; and then he had to take the state examination for Illinois. I remember hearing him tell one of his experiences with the oral part of the examination. They had all these people in bed, and they turned around and assigned one to each doctor that was taking the examination. I mean they were supposed to examine their patient; then they were to diagnose what was wrong with him. And he said he had this patient, a big husky Negro man, and he said he went over him from the top of his head to the bottom of his feet. When he got through, he told the instructor that he found absolutely nothing wrong with him. So, the instructor told him, "You're 100 percent right." He said, "He's a perfectly well man."

I remember another incident where he had a man come to his office and he diagnosed this man as having tuberculosis. When they sent him to the County Hospital and the doctors down there examined him, they sent him back home and told him there wasn't anything wrong with him. So then he came back and told Doctor what the doctors at the County Hospital had told him, and he said, "I don't care what they told you. You do have TB in the early stages." So eventually he had to go back to the County Hospital, and after that he was asked what was the name of that doctor that told him long ago that he had tuberculosis.

But you see Doctor's second wife was the one who died of tuberculosis. That was the reason why he had a great interest in that particular disease and made a special study of it. Douglas, his nephew, came down with it, and when he took sick, he went to Riverside Sanitarium and Doctor often went out to see him. He went out there and told those doctors, "This is my nephew. You got him out here and you're not doing anything for him. I want him to have the best of everything, and I do mean I want something done for him." So that's when they really started working on him. They sent him to the sanitarium way up on North Wood Avenue, and that's where he had the surgery. On that day, Doctor went to the hospital. In fact, we went to the hospital. Uncle William went right in the room and entered the amphitheater where the surgery to collapse the lung was done. That's the reason why I said he was the type of person that really was concerned about what happened to you.

Afterwards, Douglas got married to a very demanding type of woman as far as money was concerned. He had a good job and was making good money, but she kept wanting more and more. He felt so much pressure that he began to take the shoes and sell them in the streets. Well, someone told Doctor and he came down to the restaurant. That's when I was close to Doctor. I used to go up to his office and he'd call me "kid" and say, "What's the matter with you now, kid?" and I'd visit and sit there and talk with him. We were very close. Doctor and Olla used to come to our home quite often, and we'd sit down and play bridge and things like that.

So, he told Uncle Bud about what he had heard about Douglas selling more shoes outside than the man was selling inside. He was thinking that when one of us is in trouble, the whole family is in trouble. Doctor said, "I want you to go around there and talk to him about it because I think perhaps, he might take it more seriously coming from you than he would with me." Doctor did all that without any thanks. But when Doctor was sick, Douglas didn't show any love for him. So from that particular period up to the time he married, he went on his own on account of his wife and not his own accord.

Chapter 2

Brummits Moving North

Emily:

I came to Chicago in 1924, and so did Uncle William. Uncle Bud came to Chicago in February 1934. He was having marital problems. When he was in Toledo, Ohio, he got the telephone number of his brother through telephone information. He simply told them that his brother was a doctor living in Chicago. When Uncle Bud arrived, he was taken to Uncle William's home, but he was not welcomed by Olla.

I had just opened a restaurant in December 1933, and Uncle Bud was brought over to see me since he had only seen me when I was a small girl. I did not have an apartment and I was sleeping in the back of the restaurant on a day bed. He asked me that if he went back to Ohio to pick up his things, could he come and live with me and work in the restaurant. When he left, I didn't expect to see him again, but to my surprise, he returned in a few days.

The three of us —my husband and the two of us—had what you called a "hot bed." When one got out, another got in. [*Smile*] Uncle Bud and I worked the kitchen. He learned to cook well and was a great help and comfort to me. We did this for six years with no problems, and I studied his disposition and learned how to cope. He decided to go into business for himself and opened a couple of pool halls since he was a good pool player. Our restaurant business became better each day.

In a short time, I rented an apartment, and he lived with me for quite a while. Then he rented a small apartment and lived there until he moved to Robbins, Illinois, an all-black village where he bought a house. That was in 1952. He lived by himself until 1956, when I got married again and rented the house out, all except his bedroom. He did very well with the poolrooms, and he moved several times. In 1958, his health began to fail, so he sold all of his businesses and was home from then on. In 1963, he turned his house over to me in exchange for his care, and I paid the balance on his house. When he lost a leg in 1964 due to gangrene, he became so depressed that he refused to try to adjust. He remained bedfast until his death on December 17, 1965.

Chapter 3

Letters to Katherine

Houston Brummit:

If my father, Houston Whitelow, never succeeded in feeling loved by his father, Aunt Katherine fared just as poorly—but sought, at least, to capture his attention. Perhaps with the death of her brother, her only biological sibling, and tiring of her ongoing, tempestuous relationship with her father, Katherine attempted a sort of reconciliation through the intimacy of letter writing. Nevertheless, her provocative nature led her to be competitive with him, so whenever she visited her father, she was determined to beat him at tennis and bridge.

Despite Katherine's personality flaws, she was striving for independence and upward mobility. Her first residence, for example, was the 137th Street YWCA in New York City's Harlem, where many young, middle-class colored women boarded prior to securing their own apartments and homes.

Regrettably, none of her letters to her father survived, although on searching through what was left of Aunt Katherine's correspondence, I found that she had saved the beautifully written letters of Page Bell, a staff sergeant who had completed a tour of duty in Europe. Upon his discharge, he lived in Baltimore, Maryland. It is interesting to note that she last corresponded with Bell in 1949, the year her father died.

W. H. BRUMMIT, M.D.
4655 Michigan Avenue Suite 1
Residence: 5704 South Parkway

Chicago, Ill.

12/20/33

My Dear Daughter:

Your letter and card were received, and contents noted. I have thoroughly enjoyed both. I am afraid you missed the sense of my previous letter. It was not intended to portray any unhappiness, as you said, only that there is no money to be made now in the practice of medicine. In my way of seeing things, at the present time, there is nothing that shows signs of improvement in the near future. In other words, neither the NRA [National Recovery Act] nor any of the other government programs have brought any relief to the medical profession. It has simply given us worlds of work without any pay. You see the majority of folk, as well as the government, seem to think that doctors do not need consideration in their relief work and that they are simply tools to help relieve the poor sick without pay. This thing has gone so far that I believe it is going to be perpetuated because of the habit that has been indulged by the government and the people. The fact is that the large majority of people now on the relief roll have no intention of ever returning to self-support. So that is why I am saying I cannot see the end of the present situation. I am glad you see and think differently. You are not alone in your impressions. Chicago is a bustling city and I am sure if there is any comeback, she will come with the others.

You are aware of the fact of a little brown baby in the family. Now, I am sure Emily told you. Well, there was never any intention of her staying here when she came. She is the most energetic, mean little devil I have ever seen. She is now 7 months old and of course a perfect novelty, as well as a source of mirth, speculation, and concern. She dances, tries to talk, clamors for entertainment, and is never still except for very short periods of sleep. The mother is supposed to pay for her keep. However, at least, I have something to play with. I hear from the father often. He remains in fair health and says he is well cared for. He asked about you in his last letter. He also asked about the youngest boy. I had no information to give him concerning the boy because I do not know nor hear anything about him.

Will, I don't think you are so mean as folks say. Most folks will say one is mean should he or she demonstrate outwardly that they cannot be browbeaten or run over. Most of our trouble has been a want of diplomacy. We have probably used our tongues at a time when we could have covered up and yet pursued the same course without criticism.

I know many other folks who are a great deal more treacherous who are considered good. I don't think you have ever planned to hurt anyone in your life. We all may seek vengeance sometime, which is wrong but natural. I am sure you never meddled into other folks' business.

Now, for my hobby. It is Contract Bridge and I am getting a great kick out of it. Don't go chirping in with "I bet I can beat you" because I am really betting on my game and I plan my plays.

Well, I hope you're well and that you have a very Merry Xmas and that the New Year is chock full of good fortunes and happiness for you.

                                        Your Father,

                                        W. H. Brummit

Houston Brummit:

Without a large private practice and with more leisure time, Doctor permitted Olla to take in an infant, "a little brown baby," born to a member of the Orr family. By now, he could pay appropriate attention to a child, something he could not do with either Houston or Katherine.

W. H. BRUMMIT, M. D.
4655 Michigan Avenue Suite 1
Residence: 5704 South Parkway

Chicago, Ill.

7/31/35

My Dear Willie—

For some time I have planned to write you. There is a reason, just put things aside. Having been informed of your improvement made me feel so much better I decided to let myself be content with that. And the old saying that no news is probably the best news.

I am certainly glad you are getting alright again. I have seen and played against some of your rival tennis players, and I am sure you feel better for not having played me at all. However, you are not thru, I am sure.

No, I do not know the doctor you spoke of. Dr. Cooper, my office partner, or rather who is in the same suite with me, knows him.

Well, you need not be sentimental about Dad at all. He is not as bad off for change as you might think. No, I do not write him as often as I probably should. But I hear from him often indirectly and he does from me also. Don't let those things worry you.

I can never feel that those down there have ever cared much for me, not that I have done anything to them nor that they have done anything to me. We have always been different. None of them have ever taken any interest in me. Never a year passes that I do not remember him and many of the others of the family with either money or some other token.

You will be surprised to know that Dad sold his estate down there, down to the homestead and divided it among the other children and not one word did he say to me. Not that I wanted anything he or they had and would have refused any consideration at the time. Yet don't you think I should have had the chance of refusal? With the exception of Sim, I think those others would like to hear of my floating in the Lake.

Now, I did not want to write you like this, but I can very easily see your leaning. I have very great respect for my father and heaven forbid that I should do or say one thing or do anything that would even slightly hurt his feeling. I know him, but he has never known me. Not his fault, for I think he understood all the others. I shall write him soon.

I am yet well; however, that's about all I can boast of just now.

Hope you will soon be at your normal and back at your work. Hellen Wills Moody broke her back. She is going again now. Her father is a Doctor, too.

Your Father,

W.H.B.

W. H. BRUMMIT, M. D.
4655 Michigan Avenue Suite 1
Residence: 5704 South Parkway

Chicago, Ill.

8/20/35

Dear Willie:

Your letter came to me four days ago. Glad as usual to hear from you and to know that you continue to improve. Being broke puts you in the company with us all. So there is no use to worry over that. Everything is so messed up for average people that I fail to see any future. We will have to be satisfied with our daily bread, I guess.

Emy gave me a pain in the — when she wanted to come over here to spend a week or 10 days at the expense of the company   for which she works. She had no trouble in finding my address and using it without thanks or compensation. She is not telling the truth when she says she did not know my address. She could have found it at Dad's home. Besides, I had a letter from Dad and sent him some medicine. Of course, I don't give a damn about her. Only she seems to continue trying to poison your mind and make you believe I am not interested in Dad. The truth is evident. She thinks there is a little residue from the estate, and I might make some claim, which I have no intention of doing. Should I, it would be for you.

Emy may think I don't know of the hell she is responsible for previously in my home. Yet she feels so damn guilty, she uses every subterfuge to try to hide herself. I am saying this to you not because I am worrying over it, but that you may understand that I know her game. She has hit and folded her hands. A dirty coward. Her strokes have been in my book. I have often thought I would write her and enumerate the things she has done and said, most of them when she was accepting the hospitality of my home. She is void of either dignity or principle.

Now, you will please pardon me for writing you this kind of letter. I am sure you are aware of the facts in this matter.

Hoping by this time you have been able to resume your work and will soon be getting on the payroll.

I am well, although I think I am contracting a cold.

I am your Dad,

W. H. Brummit

W. H. BRUMMIT, M. D.
4655 Michigan Avenue Suite 1
Residence: 5704 South Parkway

Chicago, Ill.

4/22/37

My Dear Willie:

While sitting here and reflecting on the past with very definite plans for my future, there came into my thoughts the one and only tangible investment: "my only daughter."

You no doubt will understand the joy that came into my heart on receiving the lovely Easter card with the wording that I accepted as representing your outlook toward me. And the very beautiful lies that followed as a token also of your memory.

Well, there is very little that I can tell you of interest. The exception is that my health continues to be good, and I am making ends meet from day to day.

I do get a kick out of the little kid, Martha, we have in our home. She knows you perfectly well as her sister that lives in New York and is constantly writing and hearing from your "imaginations." She will be four years old May 1st. I wish for fun you could see her. We have not adopted her and have no intention of doing so yet. Although she was born in this home and has known no other.

You spoke something about my sizes. Well, here is my menu: Shirts 16 ¼ Sox 11 ½ Glove 10 ½. And should you want to get into the complete furnishing, my Waist, 42; Chest 44-46; Leg length 35; Arm length 36. I weigh 220 lbs. Now, that is some man, isn't it?

A few things have happened to me. Never been hurt much, tho I got stuck up once and he got $30 or $40 and my overcoat. But I didn't get hurt.

Well, spring is here now. Baseball, Tennis. There is the possibility of some swimming this summer as the pool will be across the street from home.

You can see I am yet young: the top on contract and duplicate bridge.

Nothing more, I am as ever Your Father

W. H. Brummit

Houston Brummit:

At that time, Katherine was living at 2040 7th Avenue in New York City and her father had penciled a note on the envelope: "Here is news from your loving Dad—I found a nice fellow with everything you require."

Master Sgt. Katherine Brummit, WAC

W. H. BRUMMIT, M. D.
4655 Michigan Avenue Suite 1
Residence: 5704 South Parkway

Chicago, Ill Chicago, Ill.

March 13, 1945

My Dear Sweetheart:

It is now 2 P.M., the exact time for office hours on Sundays. I have been here 2 hours. No one is in as it is "Mother's Day." I am not expecting anyone. Instead this is now your day. I am not putting off for another time as that would lead to a chance of delay.

Your letter came into the office. I opened it and before I could read any part of it, someone came in. I took the money order out and put it in my pocket without noticing the amount. I glanced at it slightly, and at the first let-up decided I would cross the street and cash it. I signed my name on the back and handed it to the manager of Walgreen's Drug Store.

He looked at me and said, "I haven't that much money on hand." I said, "What? Let me see it." And seeing the amount I said to him, "No, I don't want you to cash it now." I must show this in my office for if I go back up there with this amount of money and claim that it was from you, they will say that I was telling a lie. So, I not only showed it to the office forces, but I took it to 47th Street [his home]. Then I came in and read the letter to them to assure them it is mine to use as I pleased and not to be saved for you to call for at some future date as some of them stated.

Well, you had told me not to tell anyone. Well, I didn't. I just told everyone. I called Olla and told her, and she was very glad indeed. So you see that gift [is appreciated] not so much because of the amount but the source that has come into our life for a long time.

You see, as she stated, no one has come into our life for a long time. No one has ever given us anything. You struggle or rather take care of yourself and others. I don't think you ever expected anyone to give to us and, oh, what a pleasant surprise to us. Oh, how happy we are to know and feel that you too understand.

Mrs. Brummit, or rather Olla, has often said that someday I am going to get me some work and my very first check will be made out to you. I did not know she felt that way when she said it, but now I know. She has fully told her friends and me. I am keeping well and working like a young man. It's been a fine day here today and it's slightly cool. Now about that hand mould. When I can get the time, I'll get it for you. You can ask for the strangest things I never thought of.

Well, it is 3:40 P.M. [I'm] fast back from a call. I think I can finish my letter. I am playing bridge, mostly losing. (I did get the money in time for my regular Thursday Nite Club of four [of us]. Seven of same last Thursday Nite.) That is about the only diversion I have had yet. I am awfully tired and have been planning to get off for a few days, but things keep filling up. Several maternity cases pending, and one never knows when they are coming off. Of course, you have heard the old saying, "Make hay while the sun shines." Just now the sun is shining somewhat in my field and I am trying to gather the hay. Can't tell when it is coming again.

You will probably not need another furlough. I am thinking there is going to be quite a bit of dispensing of [the Women's Army Corps] W. A. C. duties since the war in Europe is over. I am wondering if you would like to be out. Certainly, you don't want to go to the Pacific zone of activity, do you? I know you can't say. But you can think about it. I am hoping the japs will fold up. I should think they would have enough sense to think they cannot whip the world.

I guess that is about all. I shall now go home and after dinner try to get a game that will last until about 3 AM, stay in bed until 8 AM and get to the office about 9:30. Not much work is laid out for the next or rather this week, but I am sure things will begin starting Monday morning and not tonight.

Well, so long. Many, many thanks for the big favors and the small ones that shall always be remembered. Life is now looking up where it was left off some time ago and oh, how happy I am.

Your Father

W. H. Brummit

Houston Brummit:

The acronym for the Women's Army Corps was W. A. C. Established by President Franklin D. Roosevelt, it gave home-based jobs to women and freed two million men for the armed services. At that time women were not permitted to be combat soldiers.

In his will, W. H. Brummit bequeathed $2,000 to Katherine, which was precisely the sum of money he received from her in 1945. This mean gesture, in effect, reduced her gift to him (as recorded in his letter to her dated March 13, 1945) to a business transaction requiring repayment as if between business associates. This last, enduring message to his daughter can be interpreted as a competitive, obstinate self-reliance that refused to acknowledge her gift as an act of love. For Katherine, the money she gave him was the ultimate bargaining chip for rising in her father's esteem, but in the end, he had the final word on that, too.

W. H. BRUMMIT, M. D.
4655 Michigan Avenue Suite 1
Residence: 5704 South Parkway

Chicago, Ill.

12/23/46

My Dear Sugar:

Your letter with Xmas money and contents were enjoyed and much appreciated. We have had a wonderful Xmas and everyone had plenty to eat. Personally, I have not had much time. During my vacation, I work most of the time. However, my work is not so hard now as it is limited to very few house calls and office work. Had a maternal case Friday at the hospital.

We would have enjoyed it so much to have had you here for Xmas. I was out last night for a club game. I did not win. I think Ella did. It's nice to know that you have found some comfortable home facilities. Your Democratic administration is responsible for all the mess here in politics and the people have to beg. Well, we could have my administration partially. And if we did, watch the change. Do you think you would like to have your governor for the next president or do you like Bilbo? Ha. Ha.

Well, enough of that. I can see you're getting hot under the collar. We had a card from Houston addressed to W. H. Brummit and Family. Well, we don't blame him for anything he might think or do. Although having only one grandfather, I would so much want him to learn the whole truth about me and his other constituency before it is too late. It does not hurt or disturb me at all. But when he may never know or be told the other side, it does him a great injustice. At any rate it may be possible for me to contact him before he is out of school. I will make him understand that much of his success/failure is going to be based almost entirely on his background—coming from the inherent Brummit family because there is certainly nothing on the other side to inspire or recommend.

I am very proud of you and you may be absolutely sure that you are my only. And constantly in my heart; constantly I think I am sentimental. I am just hoodwinked, and I am feeling well and not thinking of hiding my booklet. I don't go to see crazy folks nor make any suspicious calls. I drive my car carefully and I take my time.

My wants are simple and easily supplied. So there is nothing to drive me now. I simply know that boy is entirely out of line just like the other part of the family who knows the truth but try to honor themselves. I am worshipped by Reed and Emily. Those who are here know my real worth to them and what I have meant to the whole family in my accomplishments. So much for that.

We are having winter this month. Snow began to fall last nite while we were at this party. Very hard driving coming home. We were out at Lilly Clark at the same section where the Morrises lived when you were out at their party.

I am at the office. Now time is up. Home and evening off.

> Remember, I am your
> M.D. Daddie,
> W.H.B.

Houston Brummit:

I am intrigued by the way my grandfather seems to almost flirt with Aunt Katherine in his letters to her because it seems so unlike the tenor of their relationship as others described it, including Katherine herself.

Although I note in this letter how much my grandfather wanted me to "learn the whole truth," he never made the effort to write or telephone me. It was Aunt Katherine who advised me to visit him after I had spent a summer with Aunt Mildred in Detroit "learning the value of money." Instead of taking a bus home to Cincinnati, I boarded one to Chicago and arrived on September 6, 1949, the day before he died. It was interesting that Katherine had circled the third paragraph of his 1946 letter to her.

Chapter 4

The Economic Outlook for the Colored People of Chicago

(A speech written and delivered by Dr. W. H. Brummit in the 1940s)

The economic future for any group of folk in any place depends, in my way of reasoning, upon four definite points: First is the ability of those folk to satisfy their economic needs, or something that can be immediately exchanged for their needs. Second, to control or market their product. Third, the ability of the group to acquire substantial savings or holdings from the sale of their products. Fourth, the group creating an environment around these savings and holdings that can be well fitted or made to fit into the lives of their children or heirs.

Fundamentally, the first concern of any man is where and when shall I eat, where shall I sleep, and from whence will I be clothed? Of course, we don't need to stop to argue that point. That depends entirely upon the sweat of his brow.

Booker T. Washington had the vision of making labor an art rather than a commonplace drudgery; and he had a good argument when he said, "Learn to be the best workman and you will in a large way control this particular sphere." But many of us, as a group, have lived to see the fallacy of this prophesy, not only in Chicago, but everywhere else one sees buildings and monuments dedicated to that particular doctrine. Instead of this field of industry being turned over to the group, this very prophesy created a stimulus in the White Man which has grown into a most formidable competition. In other words, hard work does not always get you into the role of ownership.

Now the question is, how far if to any extent, shall the Colored Man be allowed or admitted into the skilled trades? That being the case, what is the remedy? We must eat and create. This is the problem that confronts us and must be solved by us. May I say just here in commendation of the active and successful campaign waged this last summer by *The Chicago*

Whip [newspaper]—that resulted in placing many of our groups on jobs and in making contact with some of the most highly organized industries in our country—that this will contribute in a large measure in helping to solve this problem, not only by giving jobs but the thrust must be carried further.

These Boys and Girls, Young Men and Women thus employed, should be encouraged to see deeper into their various occupations than just the jobs. In fact I am almost ready to say that those who see only the job side of the issue are hardly worth the effort. They must see far more. They should learn every detail of the Management of these enterprises in order to lay the foundation for the control and Management of similar institutions. I must suggest here that *The Chicago Whip* has hardly half done the job and should it quit here and if some movement is not put under way, and I mean in a specific way to train these Young Folks and educate them to the responsibilities of such contact, you will find yourselves in the same or worse dilemma.

The White Man has an eye that never sleeps. He stoops to conquer. You may force him into a position today and he will put you to sleep with the pretense of enjoying it, but, oh boy, when you awaken, he is far ahead. So while we have this contact, make it an incentive for future and further programs in these various fields for our group, which field we must occupy, if we are to get any place in this economic struggle. We must give up much or all of this Cod Fish Aristocracy and settle down to fundamentals. We must learn to live within our income.

Convertible assets are the great need of our group. You have heard much of bad and slow assets in the last year and no doubt, you and I have felt the effect most keenly. Some of us will continue to feel it. In our immediate vicinity, three banks have failed and brought misery to thousands of us and non-convertible assets are said to be responsible in a large measure.

It is rumored that some of these banks have failed because of premeditated fraud and criminal procedure which have been allowed to continue over a period of time and for which responsible heads of both the banking departments and officers within the institutions were cognizant for many months previous. Some quit and give up their responsibilities. Others passed the buck. Still others are granted probation. All or most of this could have been prevented by a more judicious procedure by those who knew what was going on, had they had the backbone and interest of the group at heart, rather than the personal equation.

I say again, we must have some convertible assets, and the very first of these must be character. We will never get anywhere as a group without this essential element. Character! Common and Skilled laborer, Lawyer, Doctor, Banker, Preacher or what not. The first thing that recommends you upon the road to destiny is what is your character. We must have training. This is the age of specialists; the world is calling for Masters. What I am trying to tell you is that the time has gone for the "Jack of all trades." We must pick our fields and these fields or vocations must vary with the needs of the time.

We must make special preparation to develop one's particular branch. Common labor should be diligently and honestly done. Skilled labor must be mastered. A cook, a tailor, a mechanic, a physician, a lawyer, a banker, or a preacher must learn the responsibilities of this position and meet then squarely without apology. St. Paul, a master scholar, on one occasion had this to say: "I am prepared to teach the Heathen, the Roman, and the Greek." In other words, "I have something for all regardless of race, creed, Color, or Nation. I know I have something for you, something that you need, and more to the point, something that the world can have." And I say unto you as a group, that when we make acquisitions of the things that the world needs and must have, our economic problems are then solved.

My second thought is concerning your ability to control and market or sell your product. You and I have seen Men and Women, Boys and Girls with potential abilities along certain lines, from the Prize Fighters up to the preachers, who have been denied the opportunity of development. Many have been the Inventors, the Poets, Writers, Artists, Lawyers and doctors whose fields of activity have been proscribed, but many times they were absolutely denied the opportunity to develop their line, purely for no other reason than that they were Colored. This is also true in the field of both Common and Skilled Labor. In the South, it reaches back to the farmers. In a large measure he is told what he can raise, when he can sell, to whom he must sell, and what he must get for what he sells, just what he can have, and just how he must use what he has. To disregard these orders spells destruction not only to property, but he has risked the life of himself and family. Practically all forms of labor outside of domestic have been organized and taken over by the White Man, and even Domestic Labor has been standardized: "We pay just so much."

These are cold hard facts; they are our problems not only in the South but here in Chicago. It is the duty of groups in centers like this, where we do have some chance of free speech and self- determination, to think and act for the Southern group where that privilege is denied them.

What can we do? If we could not act together, we could put at least three or four Congressmen in the U.S. Legislative Hall instead of one. There should be many more State Officials here in the North. There should be greater support to organizations like the Equal Rights League and the NAACP; from these and other similar organizations, there should come one Voice saying, "Justice and Freedom for our Group!"

We should never cease crying, fighting, and agitating until this last bar of color has been broken and our group can come before the world as other people, to control and market our wares to the world at face value.

My third thought is that our groups should have the ability to acquire a substantial savings and holdings from what it promises. As said in a previous statement, there is entirely too much Cod Fish Aristocracy among us. Too many of us have $15 hats on $1.99 heads,

$75 suits with $100 per month flats where $15 and $35 ones would more nearly suit our pocketbooks, driving Packards and Lincolns, when Fords and Chevrolets, that is, if we need a car at all, would better suit the occasion.

Too many of us are trying to make other folks think we are just things that we know ourselves not to be. And we are doing these things at the tremendous sacrifice of our present and future good. Oh! If we would only see with our eyes, hear with our ears, and profit by the many examples that are put before us each day, how different would our actions be. Note how closely the White Man, the Jew and every other race and Nationality stick to fundamentals. When you see people other than the Colored enjoying any of these expensive luxuries, you can be assured that he or they have first looked after their home; they have insurance, Bank Accounts, Securities and all the other fundamentals of economic stability.

Our Churches are given over entirely too much to the idea of acquiring a home and riches in that other World. There may be another World, but we all know we are in some kind of a World here and our comfort here depends on our economic situation. The Jew, who gave us this religion, always expected God to give them the economic advantage of other Races and Nations. Once, while under or enslaved by the Roman government, the Jews were called upon to sing some of their beautiful songs for they were considered great singers. Their reply was, How can we sing, dance, play and everything that the other group does? And yet the economic situation is becoming more and more acute. And let me say that just here, any religion or preaching that does not have for its aim the bettering of the Social and Economic Condition of the group is not the religion for me.

It is my firm belief that the economic status of any group determines, in a large measure, what their morals, their character, even their religion will be. I am not arguing that money makes character or any of these things. But I am arguing that money or the necessities of life will go a long way in stabilizing religion, morals and character. So the question, of what you have and what represents us is an all-important one. I claim it is a determining factor as to your destiny.

My fourth and last thought is the creation of an environment for the future generation that it will accept. Down South where I come from, I knew a Colored Man who had several hundred acres of land. He also owned some very good town property. He had seven Boys and three

Girls, was a great farmer, made one hundred bales of cotton each year, had horses, buggies and an automobile. He had some comforts of all kind. I would often go down to his home to shoot quail and would walk or ride on his land all day. He seemed quite satisfied and happy. This man often talked to me about his children and how he wanted each of them to have at least one hundred acres of land at his death. This man is now dead and not a single one of his children live on that place.

What was wrong? He committed one blunder after another. He let some of his boys come North; he sent all of them to school, bought them books, and they learned about Booker T. Washington, Lincoln, Frederick Douglass, Major Lynch, DuBois, Samuel Johnson, Dickens, Walter White and other immortals who helped mold sentiment in what is termed a Democratic Government, and by this means he defeated his own plans. He allowed them to learn and feel something of what freedom meant and to compare some other parts of the world with that part where they were living surrounded by a threatening mob at all times. Where he was called John, his wife Jane, and his children were called Pickaninnies by men so poor that their ribs stuck out. They could not speak a correct English sentence except when they were swearing. I am saying that if he intended to keep his children there, he committed an error in letting them see the World.

What is the status of our home life here in Chicago? Have we tried to live in and develop any center? Isn't it a fact that we are in a large measure the cause of the bank failures? The banks have been trying to finance our many new acquisitions when many of our purchases have been made on the proverbial "shoestring": $1,000 on $10,000 propositions and $5,000 on $40,000 and $50,000 properties. With large interest and prepayments none of us could possibly meet. Don't you think it would have been better for us to have developed some one single center and to have expanded as our economic conditions could control and allow? Instead we have rushed pell-mell into any and all places everywhere and anywhere the gates have been open. Oh, I do not believe in segregation as such. But since we are being treated as a group by the powers that exist, don't you think the power of concentration as a group has its advantages? Could we not have more

State Representatives? Could we not have more Congressmen? Could we not have more city representatives?

Besides, you can make a better home out of one costing $5,000 with the chance to pay for it. Our housing problem could then be solved, in accord with both our economic needs and standings. As it stands now we are faced with these conditions: first and second mortgages to be renewed, loans for taxes and improvement and other incidentals, all of which reduce our chances of ever paying for the place we call home. Now I am asking you if you believe that your children are going to attempt to assume any such burdens. No, sir. Not unless you keep them out of school in absolute ignorance.

Houston Brummit:

My own impetus to political involvement—and the beginning of my journey in civil rights participation—came from a personal experience in the sixties when I attended a stirring United Jewish Appeal conference. The keynote speaker was Margaret Mead and the UJA asked everyone for a $100 donation. At that time, I had never given such a large sum to a Jewish organization, let alone a Christian Church or the NAACP. I felt that I should first do something for the Brummit family in Camp Hill, Alabama, where one of my cousins had asked me to come and speak. As far as I could imagine, I would be carrying on the oratorical traditions of Dr. Brummit, about whom I knew very little even though I had great timidity when it came to public speaking.

I flew down to Birmingham, Alabama, where I was met by Cousin Annie Mae Bickerstaff. She drove me to Camp Hill, where I would be one of the speakers at the Murray Chapel AME Zion Church. While the church was neat, the bell tower was lying in the yard, there was debris all over the church grounds, but green grass growing in the fenced-off adjacent lot owned by whites. As I anxiously reviewed my prepared speech, the down-home preacher who went before me had all the ministerial cadence that brought "Yes, Lord" and "Amen" exclamations that made me feel as if I were in the wrong place.

When it came time for me to speak, I took a long, hard swallow and tore up my typed speech before the startled congregation. I don't remember my opening remarks, but I immediately addressed the unsightliness of the bell tower lying on the church grounds and the grassless, trash-strewn church lot. I dared to suggest that they take an active role in politics so as to shape their future so they could pave their streets and grow grass.

Members of the congregation expressed interest in running for one of the town council seats. With brashness, perhaps inherited from my grandfather, I suggested that they not just run for one council seat but all seven. Their concern was the lack of campaign funds; I offered to match every dollar they raised. Encouraged by my dare, they raised $3,169, which I matched. I later learned that this black community elected six of seven council seats. I also contributed additional funds to erect an entryway gate for the Brummitt Cemetery as a formal landmark designating the final resting places of my relatives. Aunt Zula contributed a significant amount of money, and Cousins Anna Mae Bickerstaff and Elizabeth Thomas raised the rest of the funds and engineered this project, which was completed in 1983. Having made this monetary contribution to a Negro cause, I felt more comfortable in my financial gift to the United Jewish Appeal.

The "colored" Brummit Cemetery in Camp Hill, Alabama

Part XII

Alabama's Fallen Star

Houston Brummit:

Although my grandfather had only seen me once in his life, he had little to say beyond his greeting when I, at twenty-one, made my impromptu visit to see him in Chicago. Seemingly moments later, he retired for the evening, and then died in his sleep on September 7, 1949.

There is disagreement about the exact age of William H. Brummit at his death. His driver's license lists his year of birth as 1877. If so, he would have been seventy-two at the time of his demise. If he had graduated from medical school in 1904, in his mid-thirties, he would have been at least eighty if not eighty-three in 1949. Still, the *Journal of the American Medical Association* lists his age at sixty-nine and the cause of death as coronary thrombosis and arteriosclerosis.

My nephew, Dr. Lee, found my grandfather's date of birth recorded in the 1880 United States Census, and it is listed as September 22, 1869. I have decided to resolve the mystery of my grandfather's age by relying on that year; incidentally, he missed his eightieth birthday day by just fifteen days.

William Brummit, My Physician, My Counselor, And My Friend

"WILL HE LIVE, Doctor?"

Slowly and cautiously I opened my eyes and gazed about me. I looked around, hazily, trying hard to identify the nervous voice which seemed to have floated in upon the warm Sunday afternoon breeze. Gradually, I began to see more clearly and my thoughts, in harmony with my returning vision, seemed to warn me that it was I about whom the inquiry was made. My gaze came to rest upon the handsome figure of a large white-haired man sitting very close to the couch upon which I lay. He smiled infectiously and said, "How do you feel?"

This was back in 1933 and it seems as if ages have passed since that eventful Sunday afternoon late in the month of October. The evening before I had passed out with a very severe attack of perforated ulcers, and for hours, I have been informed, I hovered somewhere between the devil and the deep blue.

Just prior to this illness, I had seen that magnificent play, "The Green Pastures," with Richard Harrison in the leading role as "De Lawd." Thus it was that when I looked into the eyes of the man who was to become not only the architect of my return to good health, but also my devoted and sincere friend, I wondered if I were dead and this stately, white-haired man of six foot three, weighing more that two hundred pounds, were "De Lawd."

How often have we enjoyed that form of nostalgia which comes with the fleeting years. During the many days of convalescence we played together—first, checkers, and he was a master; next, bridge, and he played with the same skill. Then followed long hours of political arguments. Since he was a Republican and I a political rebel, these discussions became quite heated. But, all in all, the therapeutic value can be properly assessed only by the fact that today I am well and robust.

Well, today, the doctor, my friend, my counselor, is gone. Dr. William H. Brummit—physician, scholar, philosopher, humanitarian and truly a great man—having fulfilled his mission in our society, has passed on to his reward. Surely, his reward must be likened unto the sages of old because of his beneficent and kindly treatment of his fellow man. I cannot help but feel that he was, in fact, a living symbol of the Sermon on the Mount.

Saturday morning, a few weeks ago, I sat in the chapel of Berean Baptist church as an honorary attendant listening to the last rites being held over my friend. The pastor, the Reverend C. D. L. Bradshaw, spoke with dignity and understanding. There came to assist him a pastor from Columbus, Ohio—a boyhood friend of my friend. As this boyhood chum stood on the dais looking down upon that magnificent form that once was mortal man, and related in a soft, modulated voice, their experiences as boys, men and fellow workers for a common good, my sadness disappeared. In its place came a feeling of joy. Yes, joy that I had been fortunate enough not only to have known him, but to be able to boast of his friendship. For here, lying before me, was a man who had chosen the field of medicine in which to serve his less fortunate brother.

Dr. Brummit had in every way lived the Hippocratic Creed.

Courtesy of the Chicago Defender

Part XIII

The Adopted Daughter's
Impressions of Her Father

Houston Brummit:

My interview with Martha Brummit Peters took place around 1973, and the time she spoke of was in the late 1940s and early 1950s, when desegregation of health, welfare, and education was still meeting with resistance. In Brooklyn, New York, the St. John's Episcopal Hospital, which sat in a black community, was still refusing treatment to black patients and barring black physicians from its staff. William H. Brummit's life would end in 1949, just a couple of months before the beginning of the Korean conflict.

Martha:

I saw my father as being a big noise in a small way. I just think that he gave the impression that he could be real hard—and was— but he was actually just like clay. Now, this is something that I guess I saw because I know once or twice, I said that to mother, and she said that other children didn't see him like that. Perhaps it was because I came along in his twilight years, and he had mellowed somewhat. But this is an opinion I am giving you that has to do with me and him. I don't think that he would back down from anybody, you know, outside of the house. But in the house, he was as mild as anybody could be. I remember his friend that he played bridge with, and that was usually on Saturday. I guess I believed that he got along well with other men in having witnessed this friendship.

The only frightening experience I had with him that really shook me was once when I was in elementary school. I attended the Catholic school and we had to sell these little punch cards. Mother and Dad said, "Well, we're not going to ask our friends to keep taking them every year. Some of them are not Catholic."

So, my parents paid for them and mother gave me the money. She had gotten it from my father, pinned it in my uniform, and put me in the car. He took me all the way to the Catholic school, watched me go up into the church, and I watched him drive down the street. I came back out, went across the street and bought a pickle. When I got back to the church,

I found out the money in my uniform jacket was gone. Well, I tried to decide whether suicide was the thing or if I simply should run away from home. It was weird because I had this feeling you really have when you have had it. When he came in, I was in bed because I had taken ill. He came to the bedroom and actually spanked me. He had never touched me before. This was the one time, and I was glad it was over, just like that. He didn't hold a grudge.

I don't remember my father as having a lot to do with the community unless it was something that involved medicine. The time I remember my father, maybe I was ten or twelve, was when there were so few doctors, and doctors worked real long hours. They weren't making the money like doctors make today; they got little pay. So I remember my father working long and hard. As far as I knew, he and mother used to play cards together every night. When he went out, he stood tall and was the kind of man who knew where he was going.

My father was sensitive to others. I remember when he went to the hospital for prostate surgery. I had just come home from school. Everybody went out with the stretcher and down the stairs. Mother wanted me to stay in the house and look out the window. They had gone around the corner, and I don't know how far away, when he told them that they better come back and get me. He wasn't leaving without me coming along.

I remember people telephoning and asking for Dr. Brummit. Sometimes they were the white Brummits. Then again, we would have people from out of town who thought, I guess, that he had a referral agent in the South. A couple of times people called, and they just wanted to know if it was the same Dr. Brummit that lived in Talladega. Those things still happen. Weird. You would think that by now most of the people he ever treated might be gone. I do remember he sometimes spoke with Walter White of the NAACP.

There was a patient who had had difficulty getting pregnant. The mother had just delivered, and the parents brought that baby so he could examine it. If that mother had related any concerns about her baby to the hospitals, you would never know. But I think, at that time, Negroes had to go along because there wasn't anything else we could do.

Political mentor Martha Brummit Peters greets Michelle Obama, wife of then-Senator Barack Obama, during Mrs. Obama's 2008 visit to a women's treatment center in Chicago.

There was only Provident Hospital for blacks. This is before we were on any other hospital staffs. We couldn't use another hospital. You see if you were Negro, you couldn't go to the hospital that was right across the street. You had to travel all the way down to the South Side. So you see, all the best black physicians were on the South Side. There were all kinds of things going on.

Still, white physicians would call him to the County Hospital several times because he, having come from the South, could easily identify "Southern" symptoms and conditions that were uncommon among Northerners, like pellagra. They'd never seen pellagra.

While they relied on his medical expertise to diagnose, the white hospital administrators wouldn't offer him a position on the university staff. They would just say, "Come over and tell us what this is." It was the County Hospital and the only hospital that *had* to accept us. They might not wait on you for several hours, but if you put up a fuss you could get in. Of course, at that time, patients were still segregated.

My father was a good provider. He did not have much time to talk to me because he was busy. I would see him in the late afternoons around four o'clock because he came home every day for dinner. I would see him in the mornings, but he would be sleeping.

After dinner, he would stay at home about an hour or sometimes two and then go back to his office. During those dinner times, we would sit down at the dining table together. That happened every day. On Sundays he would spend maybe four hours at the office, and the rest of the time he was at home.

He was sharp, bright, and alert. I can't think of any subject that I didn't hear my father talk about. I do know that every day he read the newspaper and we would discuss what was in the paper. Every day. He was not a drinker, but he smoked cigars.

It was late in his life that he played tennis, and I know it was about that time when he gave up making third floor calls. He was very interested in sports, way before Jackie Robinson got into the major leagues. He would go out to Comiskey Park when the Negro baseball leagues came into town and Satchel Paige was the pitcher. He would go out there all the time. He loved playing tennis, and it was later in his life when he gave it up.

He wasn't a churchgoing person, but he was a very good man, Evidently, he had gone because he was a very close friend of some minister—I can't remember his name. I do recall that there was a very prominent African minister who would visit with him, and they would retreat to have long discussions.

Now, he had a sense of humor. He was playful. I guess we would have to go back to the newspapers because he used to read *Maggie and Jiggs,* and sometimes, you know, *Maggie and Jiggs* just didn't "hit it." He would ask me something about what happened to them and all about the cartoon. I would say I didn't know. Of course, he would get a big charge out of it. Then he would find the mean barbs and explain them to me.

Houston Brummit:

Segregation in medicine existed well into the 1960s. The desegregation of American hospital training programs began in 1953, the year I graduated from Meharry Medical College. I was among the first African Americans to get an internship at the previously all-white Brooklyn Kings County Hospital. While hospital desegregation was then nationwide, in Brooklyn, this move was not due to the altruistic motives of Kings County as much as it was related to the Korean conflict and the United States military having drafted all available white male physicians, which left Kings County with newly arrived Japanese and Korean residents who could read, but not speak, English. It was also a time when Hispanic physicians were rare and white women were battling to get into previously all-male conclaves, such as surgery.

Part XIV

The Author's Impressions

Houston Brummit:

It is likely that William H. Brummit viewed my grandmother, Anna Green, his incapacitated wife, and his two young children as impediments to his attending medical school, graduating, and setting up his private practice. As a widowed, middle-aged parent, successful physician, and entrepreneur, he was convinced that providing a household staff to take care of his children was sufficient to their needs. In Olla, his third wife, he found a trusted partner in his career and financial interests. Her relationships with my father and my Aunt Katherine were dictated by her husband's own flawed relationships with his children. Her compliance in this regard allowed her to have a long, successful marriage to him.

On reconsidering my mother's perception of the "evil" Olla Brummit, I realized Olla's vulnerable position. She had been pursued by an older, wealthy professional who was determined to marry her. With the more than twenty-year age difference and her comparative naiveté, she was invited into a union that honored her with a marriage to a doctor, a social status that few Negro women at that time would have experienced. Yet, unbeknown to her—and William—she would be entering a union that had doomed his previous marriages: as a carrier of tuberculosis, William, inadvertently, had infected his susceptible wives; he himself was immune. Fortunately, Olla proved to have a resistance to the fatal germ, but once she married, she was immersed into a complicated, dysfunctional family and was bound to make mistakes.

But he is not so easy to empathize with. My mother remembered the day of my father's funeral in 1930 in Cincinnati, where my grandfather made an appearance, stepped over me, two years old at the time, and barely expressed his condolences to her. Despite this occasion being the only time when three generations of W. H. Brummit's family were together, he left as quickly as he could the next day.

I can only surmise that on one level, William was a child who had never grown up. With his own need for validation, he saw children as his competition or, like the Victorians, as little adults, somewhat self-contained and self-reliant. He did not realize the need for children to be nurtured and encouraged. It may have been that his own childhood, one that must have been centered on strenuous, backbreaking farm labor, formed his personal philosophy regarding children. As the first child and oldest son, William Henry Harrison was most likely saddled with arduous responsibilities at   a very early age. It is probable that his memories and resentment incited a callousness that was manifest in his interactions with his own children.

His relationship with Olla, however, was very different. When Olla spoke of herself and Dr. Brummit, she seemed always to be in the realm of idyllic romance, precisely recalled. She was able and willing to sustain this somewhat fairy-tale version of her marriage largely by succumbing to William's insistence that she remove herself from the children's affairs. Without an engaging maternal figure in their lives, it is no wonder, then, that Houston and Katherine were in emotional crises.

For example, in 1933, Katherine had severe issues that came together and undermined her emotional equilibrium. First was the introduction of Martha into the family by her stepmother. Given the safe distance between Chicago and New York, the advent of Martha dethroned Katherine as the object of her father's affection, for no longer was she the only daughter. Although he seemingly shared his inner feelings with Katherine, he signed his letters to her with the formal, maybe even impersonal, "W. H. Brummit." The total acceptance of Martha by her father engendered Katherine's rage, for which there was no outlet other than turning it inward into a depressive episode.

Second was the parental neglect that began with the early death of her mother. She was left first on the Brummitt farm, and then with the various housekeepers who took care of the home in Talladega while her father was busy establishing his practice and, as a "ladies' man," courting. Essentially, her father was a distant parent and an inconsistent role model. He never allowed himself to have emotional contact with Katherine and Houston except on an ad hoc basis, usually confined to paying their bills and disciplining them.

Imprinted by her father's disaffection, Katherine manifested traits of Borderline Personality Disorder (BPD). According to the *Diagnostic and Statistical Manual of Mental Disorders* (fourth edition), BPD is a pervasive pattern of marked impulsivity and instability in interpersonal relationships, self-image and affects that begins in early adulthood. A person diagnosed with BPD experiences intense abandonment fears and inappropriate anger even when faced with realistic, time-limited separation or when there are unavoidable changes in plans. However, Katherine may also have been a bit histrionic. The following account reveals the coolness that both Olla and William demonstrated when Katherine was most likely experiencing a BPD episode:

Olla:

As I said before, Katherine had moved down the street to somebody's house, across the street from the hospital. I never did bother with his children, and I never fussed or fought with them. They were always mad about something that I never knew about. Because he didn't want me to bother him about his children, I never did.

It was about 1934, a year before their grandfather died. Doctor got some kind of message to come to New York City at once. Willie was sick in hospital. At the time, he wasn't feeling too good, and he wasn't one of those men who liked to travel across the world. So he told me that something had happened to Willie and he didn't feel like going. He wanted me to go see her. Because Emily and I were good friends, she wanted to go with me. Josephine was working at a hospital in New Jersey. I called her up, and she went with us to Bellevue Hospital. When we got there, Willie wasn't there anymore, and we drove out to her home. The man who owned the house was dead. A woman who lived there said Katherine was always having these blow-ups and going to pieces. At this particular time, she had blown up at somebody so badly that Katherine, herself, decided she was sick. So, she went to Bellevue for a rescue.

After we drove to the next place, some doctor asked me to come into the office and he began to ask me many questions. You see, I didn't know what she had told him, and he told me a whole lot of stuff she had said that I didn't even know about. He just asked me all these questions, and I just denied them all because I had never heard about these things. We spent the day out there with her, and she seemed normal. But Willie was always like that: all right today and cracked tomorrow.

Houston Brummit:

As a physician, her father must have suspected that she had psychiatric problem. As a father, he might have been embarrassed or felt guilt, particularly if her "condition" was inherited by her from him. In any case, the cause he did not want to acknowledge—or claim responsibility for, and the way he coped with Katherine was to keep emotionally aloof from her. In doing so, he restrained a parental tendency toward love, support and encouragement. He primarily wanted to wish her well but without getting too involved.

Certainly, her father played a role in creating her Electra complex, which is the Oedipus complex when it occurs in a female. Eventually, she fell back on good judgment and an instinct for survival. Katherine managed to graduate from college, succeed at civil service employment, save her money, and always move toward middle-class housing. In her senior years she placed herself in the Kittay House, a brand-new Bronx residential facility for seniors who wanted independent living.

Whenever my questions were steered toward the subject of my father and Aunt Katherine, Olla's memory faltered. It seemed she had to be reminded that certain events even occurred. She may have been projecting the perspective of Dr. Brummit, a man who clearly valued education and had the financial resources to pay for the college tuitions of his children but chose not to. Olla herself couldn't explain why Katherine had to pay her own way through Wilberforce University. Nor was there an explanation for why Dr. Brummit did not take charge of the health needs of his only son, who was ill with tuberculosis and would eventually die of it but would later take such great pains to save the life of an unappreciative nephew.

The many unanswered questions regarding Dr. Brummit's familial relationships leads me to move away from the domestic sphere to the national. It is here where, I believe, my grandfather wanted to excel and could have excelled, but he was born, perhaps, a century too soon. His visionary speech reveals future realities that are currently impacting the economic health of this nation.

When reading my grandfather's speech, I can't help but acknowledge how applicable his message is today. One must also wonder how, for all he had gone through, having lost his status and success, his tenor could be so uplifting, practical, and courageous, and reflect no bitterness over his plight.

Given the complications of the time, I am mindful of my grandfather's own challenges, attempting to realize his sizable ambition in a racial climate that ultimately suffocated its promise. He had become a threat to spiteful whites in Talladega: The United Klansmen of America had already burned down the small black town of Rosewood, Florida, on New Year's Day, 1923—the year before the 1924 abduction and assault of my grandfather. It is in the context of such a racially divided society that one must see both his strengths and his weaknesses.

The only Talladega College archival evidence of Dr. W. H.
Brummit's NEW ERA PHARMACY is this undated, haunting interior.

Notice his name appearing through the window.

Part XV

Epilogue

For reasons of his own, my grandfather had his mind fixed on settling in Talladega, where indeed, he built up a lucrative practice and became a prominent civic leader. Had he chosen to practice medicine in a larger urban venue such as Birmingham, Alabama, he would probably have done just as well in his profession, but it is interesting to ponder his reception—and acceptance—among the rising ranks of the black middle class.

I can only imagine that his refusal to transplant himself out of the rural, agricultural society into which he was born was due to his awareness of his own social vulnerability. Would he have been able to "fit in" with refined society? Had he encountered taunts and teasing from medical students at Meharry whose educations and family backgrounds were considered more impressive than his? Was there something about him that was too innately "country" or uncouth and defied taming? Talladega, then, shielded him from the likelihood of experiencing humbling situations due to his unfamiliarity with the social graces and urban social scene.

Talladega functioned not only as his social protector but catapulted his career and reputation. The small town showcased his talents and allowed his ambitious nature to flourish, but as a big fish in a little pond, Dr. Brummit failed to factor in the consequences of calling attention to himself, whether by accident or design, specifically by his monopolizing presence in the area of surgery. The twenty- one bed E. A. Goodnow Hospital where he conducted his surgical practice probably came to symbolize "Doctor" and his uncanny ability to overcome both physical disease and the disease of racism, for he viewed himself as not merely on par with but *superior* to the white doctors whom he encountered. My grandfather's surgical confidence or arrogance (as some might deem it) was undeniably underwritten with competent execution, but in a small Southern town, his success and overexposure would later make him a target of friend and foe alike.

One of the casualties of my grandfather's exile from Talladega was the nursing program. In April 1926, exactly two years after the KKK assault, the college trustees voted to discontinue the nursing program.

The first floor of the Goodnow building became a college infirmary, administered by nurses. It continued in that capacity until 1974 and the opening of the Voorhees Infirmary in another building. After 1974 the Goodnow Hospital building was used as a preschool and art studio. Major renovations took place during 1980-1981, adapting the building to the needs of the college art program.

It's worth noting that the E. A. Goodnow Hospital was the only hospital in Talladega until 1943. The white city administrators of Talladega later purchased the Alabama Synodical College building which they improved and expanded into the Citizens Hospital, where they developed a nursing program. Although white citizens brought about the demise of the E. A. Goodnow Hospital, it's ironic that hospital care at Talladega College under the auspices of Dr. Brummit and E. A. Goodnow was nearly four decades ahead of the white citizens of Talladega.

Perhaps the most important issue here is not what Talladega offered my grandfather but what it couldn't: worthy competition. In not having medical peers whom he respected and with whom he could engage in challenging discourse, Dr. Brummit, in effect, was limited in terms of expanding and advancing his own medical skill and knowledge. He was dismissive of Drs. Jones and Brothers—as he was of his wannabe younger siblings—but a formidable colleague would have led to a dynamic contest of medical strategies and treatments from which the patients and the profession would have benefited. It may have been that if he had relocated to Birmingham, he would have had intellectual repartee and support from the empathetic white Dr. Wheeler as well as black colleagues to help him advance in the profession.

In addition to enjoying a hometown comfort zone and professional prestige, it is probable that my grandfather's wealth and Talladega success blinded him to the obvious threat he engendered by encroaching on the financial fiefdoms of white businessmen. As with any person making large sums of money in a community where he has little competition, Dr. Brummit began to feel a certain amount of invincibility. In this instance, a prominent black surgeon practicing medicine in segregated Alabama was able to bank tens of thousands of dollars. By 1910, the *only* hospital in Talladega had been built on the *black* Talladega College campus to provide an arena for Dr. Brummit to perform surgery. Until 1943, whites had to go to Birmingham or elsewhere to receive competent treatment.

Later, his forced exile north was a traumatic leap into oblivion, for even after acquiring an Illinois state medical license, he was not accepted as the surgeon he had been. Chicago had its own apartheid, and Negroes did not have the medical privileges enjoyed by white physicians. While twenty-five years of sitting in Chicago medical offices gave him time to prepare speeches and to write eloquently, his letters to Katherine demonstrate the petty fixation on archaic entitlements that followed him to his grave.

The person I saw on the last day of his life was a frail, elderly man who had recently undergone surgery and was very much bound to the chair in which he sat, not the proud, robust force of a man who boasted of jumping tennis nets at the age of seventy-five. He was also not the fabled figure who had led the mixed-race community of Talladega through his medical practice and bold entrepreneurship. I am mindful of how time rounds the edges of memory. While my mother fiercely denounced this man who had failed to support or encourage his children, I can now also see a deeply conflicted figure, certainly flawed in his personal values, but also born in a time and place that would cripple his ability to realize his considerable ambition.

W. H. Brummit was a father who failed his children in many ways, and they certainly paid a price for that. But in his Talladega days, he was a legend, an enterprising leader in his community, and an inspiration to the many friends and patients who remembered him long after he left.

In my efforts to discover William Henry Harrison Brummit, I relied on family sources and the college wherein he gave so much of himself. His family, particularly his wife, Olla, provided some enlightenment, but when I contacted the head librarian and campus nurse at Talladega College on October 22, 2008, it was my hope that I would learn more fully of my grandfather's contribution to the E. A. Goodnow Hospital and the college. Imagine my amazement and disappointment to find that neither had heard of my grandfather nor his once popular off-campus ice cream parlor. While Drs. Brothers, Jones, Salter, and Wren could all be located in the archives of Talladega College, it seems as if Dr. Brummit exists only as hearsay, a ghostly spirit among his deceased, yet remembered, colleagues. In the professional arena, my grandfather does not even appear as a footnote.

The disconnect between my family's vivid recollection of him and the college's near-total forgetfulness leaves me pointing an accusatory finger at the Ku Klux Klan for instigating the disappearance of my grandfather from Talladega history. After my grandfather's abduction, I am sure that worried, "embarrassed" administrators must have viewed him as a threat, liability and taint to Talladega College's emerging status. Here is a case where the victim is further victimized. Administrators must have fretted about continuing monetary support from benefactors, particularly the American Missionary Association. If so, Talladega College had to make the difficult choice between the approval of the white populace or a black surgeon, a city or a man. The city won, and the victim was further victimized. But with the Klan's effective erasure of Dr. Brummit from the annals of this historic college, my grandfather becomes more legend than man, and in that, at least, I have some satisfaction.

Acknowledgments

I extend my gratitude to Talladega College and staff members, *Juliette Smith* (College Library Director) who uncovered the few surviving articles about my grandfather as well as the original pictures of the E. A. Goodnow Hospital where he had performed surgery and *Valerie Alfred* (Dept of Student Affairs) for sharing with me her memories about the unused, second floor operating room and its ancillary equipment.

Personally, I am indebted to my friend, *Francis Polizio,* who dedicated several months of his time to the first edition of *TALLADEGA DAYS,* and *Karen Watts* my first editor from IUniverse for her initial developmental efforts in shaping the book.

Thanks to the collaborative talents of professional execution in their specific areas of expertise: graphic designer *Sarah Gager* of Sarah Gager Design Studio; *David Benbennick,* map locator; *Greg Scott,* graphic and photographic services; copy editor *Vicky Wilson-Schwartz; Linda Wallace* of Linda S. Wallace Communications, for securing permission from the Chicago Defender for use of archival newspaper articles and Attorney *Sandra Aya Enimil*, Intellectual Property Manager, Chicago Defender Newspaper, whose diligence retrieved the startling front-page headline that underscores the significance of my grand-father's assault to Black journalism and history.

I owe so much to the tireless participation and coordination of *Theresa Marsh*, my friend and editor who elevated the second edition of *TALLADEGA DAYS, Race Rural Life, and Memories of a forgotten Legend and KKK Survivor* to professional standards and *Scottie Lee Davis* for her research, editing and data entry for this final 2021 edition of *TALLADEGA DAYS, the Life of William H Brummit, M.D., Civil Rights Activist, Forgotten Legend and KKK Survivor.*

My final words of gratitude are directed, to my family, a cast of dynamic personalities who created a past worth investigating and particularly William H. Brummit, M.D., my grandfather. It is with the hope that the reader will recognize, appreciate, and honor the life paths of those in their own families who have come before.

A 2012 photographic portrait of author Houston Brummit

Born and reared in Cincinnati, Ohio, Houston Brummit attended black elementary schools until he entered Walnut Hills High School. Upon graduating in the 11th grade at age 16, he entered the University of Cincinnati. His last two years were spent at Wilberforce University, an all-black school in southern Ohio. While pre-Med in orientation, he wrote and produced variety shows and discovered the passion for telling a good story.

Houston, like his grandfather who graduated 49 years before him, entered Nashville's Meharry Medical College. After graduation and two years in the United States Air Force, he pursued adult and child psychiatry at Bellevue and New York University hospitals, later becoming board certified in both specialties. On establishing a private practice, he was the Judas goat used by Congress of Interracial Relations to desegregate much of New York housing.

In 1962, he continued his passion for theatre and was one of the first persons of color to produce and Off-Broadway play (a spoof of *A Raisin in the Sun*, entitled *Raising Hell in The Sun*). This accomplishment opened the gates for several black actors and other creatures of theater to receive admission to the Actors' Equity Association, giving them access to more work in the industry.

Dr. Brummit is a lifetime member of the National Association for the Advancement of Colored People and lifetime fellow of the American Psychiatric Association and a member of the Dramatist Guild, a playwright organization. For many years he was active with the Latin American Theatre Ensemble and as a board member of the Richard Allen Center for Culture.

Houston Brummit is retired and resides in New York City. In addition to professional articles, he has written an assortment of musical dramas and plays including *Makin It, Theatre of Suggestion, Too Late for Tears,* as well as published novels entitled *Meshuggah?* and *Talladega Days*.